HELP!
I'm Having a Miscarriage

Bishop Joseph Hall Jr.

"Making Spiritual Decisions during Debilitating Life Conditions can bring you a Life of Unlimited SUCCESS!"

Help I'm Having A Miscarriage

Author: Bishop Joseph Hall Jr.

Executive Editor: Besty Rosario

Cover Design: Elroy Forbes

Cover Photo: Sederek Smith

Copyright © 2018

ALL RIGHTS RESERVED. No part of this work covered by the copyright herein may be reproduced, transmitted, stored or used in any form or by any means of graphic, electronic, or mechanical including, but not limited to photocopying, recording, scanning, digitizing, taping, web distribution, information networks or information storage and retrieval systems, except as permitted under Section 107 or 108 of the 1976 United States Copyright Act, without prior permission of the author. To obtain permissions to use content from this work, please submit written request to

ISBN- 978-0-9981777-4-8 Paperback 978-0-9981777-5-5 hardcover

Biblical references used derive from King James Version, New International Version, and English Standard Version.

Go'Judah Pushing Company 1-855-GOJUDAH

Help | *I'm Having a Miscarriage*

The "Help" Book of Life

Special thanks to these precious people to invested into this book project to make it a reality!

Kim Davis	Charice Hensley
Cathy Evans	Ricky & Denal Chambers
Charles & Valarie Bratchett	Regina Samuels
Thomas & Wilma Drain	Jimmy Hogan Jr.
Nettie Whitaker	Latosha Wyatt
Gloria Young	Ruby Cherry
Charme Williams	Deborah Faye Avery
Willie French	Herbert & Janice Edwards
Yolanda Dewberry	NeKeshia Sloan

Table of Contents

Chapter 1:   We All Need Help To Succeed...8

Chapter 2:   Conception Is Necessary Before Manifestation......................19

Chapter 3:   Pregnant With A Purpose..40

Chapter 4:   Someone (GOD) Partnered With Me To Form This Baby.......52

Chapter 5:   Help Developing the Baby..69

Chapter 6:   Spirit vs Soul..81

Chapter 7:   Symptoms of A Miscarriage...93

Chapter 8:   "Panic Attack"...107

Chapter 9:   Help So I Can Deliver My Baby..115

Chapter 10: Help Me Communicate Better..123

Chapter 11: I Can Do This..132

Chapter 12: I Won't Let GOD Down..149

Chapter 13: I Am What I Am By The Grace of GOD..............................155

Chapter 14: The Challenge of Birthing A Blessing..................................158

Chapter 15: Prenatal Praise..167

INTRODUCTION

YOU WERE BORN WITH A PURPOSE!

Do not be alarmed! You have the right book in your hands. If you have ever experienced trials, tragedies and failures, that placed your GOD given purpose at risk, this book is for you. If you are at a point in your life where you are at the edge of giving up, because of life's way of mishandling you, again, this book is definitely for you. Each of us are here for a reason and being **"purposed"** makes it practically impossible to simply exist. However, fulfilling that purpose is hard work. It comes with a multiplicity of oppositions and adversities. Nevertheless, GOD has placed within each of us, an arsenal of tools and weaponry that will assist us in fulfilling purpose and destiny.

The concept of carrying purpose is very similar to the concept of pregnancy. In pregnancy there are certain measures that need to be taken, for the baby to be born healthy. There are nine months of hormonal changes, physical transformation and more. It is an intricate process that brings forth a beautiful result; **that is, *if the woman escapes the high-risk stages of miscarriage***. A miscarriage is defined as, *"a natural loss of the products of conception; spontaneous abortion or stillbirth."*[1] Basically, a miscarriage is when a pregnant woman loses the baby (*death*); while it is yet in her womb. The idea of miscarriage symbolizes distress, loss and failure. A miscarriage also carries with it, potential health

---

[1] (Merriam-Webster 2010)

risks for the mother; both physically, emotionally and psychologically.

This book doesn't really focus on physical miscarriages. In this book the motif of miscarriage does deal with distress, loss and death. Yet, it is used to compare the duress, misplacement and dissolution that may attempt to threaten our purpose. When we lose sight of our purpose due to circumstances that occur in various phases of our life, we too are exposed to significant risks.

The focus of this book is to delve into the process of learning how to make sound decisions, during critical phases in this life; that will prevent spiritual miscarriages. Situations that affect our spiritual life may endanger our effective use of the gifts of the Holy Spirit; which may lead to unbelief, weak faith or backsliding. This is the reason that GOD left us resources to help us carry the purpose, in which he placed within us, to full term. Though we may encounter obstacles; we are equipped with all the help that we need, all we must do is, access it.

Philippians 4:13 proclaims that, *"I can do all things through Christ who strengthens me"*[2]. This happens to be one of the most confessed Bible passages, but sometimes the one that is not truly believed by most. We must believe that we can really do all things through Christ. Our help comes from GOD who made Heaven and Earth. It's by His grace that we are here, and His grace is sufficient to make us who we are called to be and produce the purpose that He

---

[2] Philippians 4:13 NIV

predestined us to carry out. Understand this, there is no harm in seeking help from Christ Himself; even if we feel it's undeserved. In one of his publications, *Become A Better You*, Pastor Joel Osteen stated, *"You needn't go through life with that nagging feeling;- "GOD is not pleased with me. I'd be a hypocrite to ask for His help after all the mistakes I've made"*[3]. GOD's resources are available to us.

There are no promises of a perfect life, but we have the perfect source. Regardless of the risks associated with carrying purpose, miscarrying is not an option for those of us that are called, chosen and destined for greatness. You and I may face setbacks, but we must stand firm on the words written in Jeremiah. GOD has plans for you. He has a purpose for your life and wants to see you succeed. Take this journey with me as I share with you, my story. Don't give up! Don't surrender to your circumstances, because there is a solution. There is resolve. It all begins with a purpose driven and spiritual mindset. [4]You must focus on those things before you and press on toward that higher call; which is in Christ JESUS.

---

[3] OSTEEN 2012
[4] King James Version - Philippians 4:13

Chapter One

We All Need Help To Succeed!

When we entered this world, we all entered under different circumstances. Whether our mother had a C-section or pushed us naturally down her birth canal, we all needed assistance in getting here. If you were born before the 90's like me, it's a great possibility that once you made your arrival, the doctor held you upside down and gently smacked you on the bottom. This medical practice was not done to harm the baby, but to help it gain it's very first breath. If the baby cried out, this was a positive sign to everyone that the baby was alive!

Now, let's compare that analogy to our life in Christ. Each of us came to Christ under different circumstances. Despite the differences, none of us can take this walk alone. Think about the moment that you surrendered your heart to Christ. I can recall my own experience. Although I was young, I was offered the right hand of fellowship in a powerful, Holy Ghost filled church service. I was not alone and others rejoiced in my new birth into the body of Christ.

Similar to a newborn baby, we come into our faith walk needy and dependent; solely relying on GOD to help us live purposefully. [5] The bible states, "...*if any man be in Christ, he is a new creature: old things are passed away; behold, all things are become new.*" Because we have become "*anew,*" we must seek help in order to fulfill our purpose. The great thing about it, is that, we don't have to look too far to find help, because GOD sent His son and the Holy Spirit. **GOD established Help for us before we were ever born.**

[6]Science shows that the full cycle of life is goes from the prenatal, infancy, toddler, preschooler, grade schooler, teen, young adult, adult and then into senior citizen hood. Of all the different phases of development, the most miraculous phase to me is the prenatal stage.

This process intrigued me so much, that I phoned a doctor and close friend of mine to get more clarity on the process. He began like this, "*Imagine this: when a female egg gamete (ovum) combines with a sperm gamete it forms a zygote. Then, the zygote divides rapidly into two identical cells called blastomeres during a process that is termed, cleavage. Afterwards, the cells divide again; while traveling along the fallopian tube to get to the uterus. After the diploid zygote arrives in the uterus, it officially starts the germinal stage. Then, pregnancy happens!*" Now, if you are like me, the

---

[5] King James Version
[6] WebMD-https://www.webmd.com/parenting

extensive medical vernacular that my friend used had me a little lost. Let me clarify: byway of sexual intercourse or insemination the female egg is fertilized by the male's sperm. Then, the fertilized egg journeys to and attaches to the uterus wall; there life begins.

What a miraculous and intricate process to think about. The most astonishing aspect for me, is seeing the meticulous nature of GOD in this process. Then, the Holy Spirit spoke to me saying, *"Do you see how important you are to me?"* It is amazing to think that GOD loves us so much, that He would orchestrate each, tiny facet of our being and attach to that, **purpose**. You are so significant that the insignificant hairs that you involuntarily shed and leave in your brush or shower daily *are all numbered. Don't be afraid; you are worth more than many..." (Luke* 12:7, NIV).

When we take a closer look at the Greek meaning of zygote, we will discover that the term means, *"yoked."* This is a great place to highlight; it is the zygote that carries both parents' genes. They possess every essential element needed for development, within its DNA. It is the factor that determines the characteristics of the developing organism.

Isn't it amazing how GOD in his infinite wisdom already predestined the process it would take to get us here? Neither of our parents had to instruct their bodies on any of the steps for us to get here. Now, there was work involved, but GOD made the process easy. **GOD so designed it that He has already encrypted our purpose with success.** Our purpose has all the essential elements needed to properly develop. All we need to do is yield ourselves to

Him and watch Him cultivate us into what He has purposed for our life.

The creation, as detailed in the book of Genesis is another great example of GOD's predestined order and establishment of help for humanity! He knew what was needed in the earth to ensure man's survival and He simply spoke that into existence. From the great Texas pines, massive and tiny bodies of water, to exotic fruits, plants and animals; all that we need for proper living is here. **What we call nature is GOD's provision; His aid to us.** Adam and Eve didn't have any problem with living because The Creator was their help. Even after the fall of man, GOD became the first tailor for our sake. The relationship ripped by Adam's disobedience and Eve's naivety was "*cross-stitched*" back together on [7]Gûlgaltâ's hill; providing you and I a chance to get things right in our own lives.

Redemption and salvation were two of the greatest gifts that GOD prepared for us, prior to our birth. David detailed it best in Psalm 51 that we are, *"... born in sin and in inequity shaped..."* Okay, David did not mean babies are born sinning, but it was a sincere confession of his own sinful heart to GOD. Over two thousand years ago, the greatest help we would ever receive was born into this world. That hand of help was not meant only for those alive during JESUS's time. His sacrifice was for everyone before and after Him. Those who saw JESUS in the flesh had the

---

[7] Golgotha, (Aramaic: "Skull") called Calvary, (from Latin calva: "bald head," or "skull"), skull-shaped hill in Jerusalem, the site of JESUS' Crucifixion.
https://www.britannica.com/place/Golgotha.

opportunity to receive salvation directly from Christ, physically and spiritually. We all can embrace salvation.

If we know that help existed before we were born, then why do we fail to tap into the greatest privilege that we have? It still puzzles me. It would be like someone wanting to live without ever eating or drinking. A life without utilizing the bare necessities, isn't a life. Let's look a little deeper into the *spiritual* birthing process and what is needed, so that you avoid miscarrying your purpose.

The Birthing Process

One of the greatest wonders of humanity is the birthing process. Whether it is birthing a new vision for our family, relationships, career, business, church, or for our personal life; it is important that we all learn how to embrace the gift of help.

We are daily living out our story and every chapter will not be filled with sunshine and smiles. Being on top of the world isn't an everyday experience. Some chapters in our story reveal our human struggles, fears, doubts, hurts and pains. I am convinced that there are many stages that lead to our success. One can obtain success, but not without any lessons (failures). One cannot birth greatness, without going through some level of discomfort; thus, my analogy of giving birth. I believe that this process helps give to us a more relevant point of reference by which we can identify as we strive to reach full our potential.

For some, the birthing purpose may be starting a foundation and feeding thousands of people around the world. Maybe, you're one of the greatest business minds of our day and you have an invention that can improve the way humanity lives. For others, it may be being a caretaker of your community and having a dream to get at-risk youth, off the streets and into productive programs that will give them life skills. You may be a spiritual leader who wants to take church beyond the four walls, developing better ways to help serve your community and abroad. Whatever you have in your heart to become or to accomplish, it will not be an easy task to achieve, nor a guaranteed success. You will have to do your part by being open to GOD's plan and following His lead to your destiny.

You are pregnant with Purpose, don't miscarry your baby!

We have established the fact that you can't have success without lessons (failures). You cannot birth greatness without going through some level of discomfort. No pain, no gain. No joy without sorrow. Even though sorrow is temporary sometimes that joyful morning takes too long to come. Well, what can we do when discomfort and failures come? **Seek Help!**

No Pain No Gain

Everyone wants success in some way or another, but not everyone wants to endure the process that it may take to get there. The temperamental *"microwave"* mindset of this culture has programed many to believe that we can reach success overnight or without any struggle, but that is far from the truth. The microwave mindset believes that one can simply place their dream in a high voltage, radioactive amped contraption and dreams are ready after a few minutes. Yes, we have seen times when people win the lottery and instantly become rich, but they never share how many hundreds or thousands of dollars they spent prior to getting that winning lottery ticket. It is easy to look on the surface and assume something is easy. However, you may not always know the struggle that came before the success.

I was taught by my parents, early in life that if anything was worth having, you must work for it. This same lesson is one that I have passed down to my own children. Being able to obtain success in every area of your life will take setting goals, preparation, hard work, prayer and faith.

During the summer, our church normally takes our youth on a getaway, summer trip. It is during this time that I get to ride and converse back and forth; during the long drives to our destination. My attempt is to observe and simply get eye level, face to face and inside the youth's mind; through conversation. I take time to pick their brains, just to see how they were thinking. I asked some of the kids what they wanted to be when they grew up. Like the typical child, they would rattle off the same common professions such as: a lawyer, a doctor, an NFL football player and teacher. To my surprise, one young boy said, *"a Pastor."* Oh, how that made me smile. In that moment, *I was reminded that someone was watching me.* I then asked them what plans they had set in place to ensure their success. Some said they would go to college, others shouted that they would work hard in sports. Then, that same little boy who just stated that he wanted to be a preacher, looked up at me. His intuitive statement slid out through the sly grin on his face, *"Pastor, I changed my mind because I don't like funerals. If I become a pastor, then I will have to be around dead people and I fear dead people!"* Everyone in earshot distance erupted with laughter including me. I comforted him by saying that "GOD will prepare you, to be able to handle everything that comes with your assigned purpose. So, don't fear, but have faith in GOD."

    Having this quality time with the youth was really important to me as a leader. Even at that moment I was able to connect with some of the future leaders of faith in my community. As a pastor and leader in my community I believe we should embrace our youth and get to know them. They are the church of today and tomorrow. If we invest most of our time in the older generation and sit idle in helping develop our youth; we are forfeiting an amazing opportunity to help forge a successful path, future and legacy for the church. Neither do I want our youth to grow up believing that they are not valued, nor do I want them believing that they can have success without setting goals and working for what they want. There are times I volunteer with other youth in the community or at the local school. It really saddens my heart sometimes, just to observe how this generation has a stronghold of entitlement. Many feel like they deserve what they want simply because they want it. This mindset is detrimental to purpose and could be a factor that contributes to a miscarriage. I believe that when society feed into this unhealthy ideology, we are setting our own community up for failure.

Does an aspiring student who has a desire to become a doctor, just show up to medical school and get a license to practice medicine overnight? No, not in our society. Those of us who have been through several transitions in life understand the importance of going through a tried process. We understand that making it through the process is a clear sign of confirmation to us and others that we are prepared and ready to achieve greater. The reality and danger to those who believe the myth that success comes without a process or a price, is that life kicks in and too often, they cannot handle the outcome. Therefore, this perception places some of the most gifted people in a debilitative state. Because of this, they tend to suffer with anxiety, low self-esteem and or depression; as they live in a constant state of fear, questioning the reality of their potential. What's wrong with me? Do I really have what it takes to succeed? Why can't I have success now? This is another reason why writing this book was imperative to me. After being on this earth a little over fifty years, I have gained some insight and wisdom from life's many lessons. Truthfully, those lessons are what helped me gain success and access to unlimited wealth. I dare not withhold what I have gained and not reach back to help others do the same.

One of humanity's greatest teachers, Maya Angelou put it best, she said, *"When you learn, teach, when you get, give."* This statement of wisdom reigns true in my life. Almost everyone that I know who lives by this principle, has obtained success in their lives.

After looking back over my life, I can think of the many people who helped me along the way. Each phase of my life brought new challenges, but each shift prepared me for the next.

It is crucial for you to understand this concept; getting assistance that is needed is not wrong. Getting help should not be viewed as a negative thing. Helping is one facet of love and to know love is to know GOD. Our creator has showcased love to all of us, I'm reminded of the scripture, *John 3:16, "For GOD so <u>love</u> the world that <u>He gave</u> his only begotten Son, that whosoever <u>believe</u> in him shall not perish but have everlasting life."* This text announces the unlimited love that our creator has for us.

GOD sent us help because He knew we would need it. In His good fatherly fashion our needs were His priority. He didn't just send us any kind of help, He sent His absolute best. JESUS, His only begotten son was sent as a sacrifice to show us how to live the best life. In retrospect, this is also GOD's way of teaching us reciprocity. He modeled for us that when we help others, we are operating in his likeness of love. Also, when we receive help with appreciation and humility we are operating in his likeness.

You may believe it or not, but during the getaway summer trip, the youth didn't discover who or what they wanted to become at the moment that I asked them. They had previous knowledge of that purpose. That young man who wanted to become a pastor like me must have thought about it, long before making his decision. When the issue of funerals came into the equation, his purpose was on the verge of miscarriage; just within minutes. Nothing good comes easy, we need to work for it.

As we continue, we will explore the benefits of being pregnant with a spiritual purpose, *(having a call of ministry on your life)*. As we explore, I will;

- further elaborate on **developing** the Baby *(ministry)*,
- **Help** identify the Symptoms of a **miscarriage**,
- Assist with **delivering** the baby,
- Give you tools to successfully raise the baby.

These key points are vital, understanding them will help you to become more aware of your GOD given purpose and how best to develop it. But before we go deeper, here is my sincere prayer to The Father on your behalf: *"I pray that you learn how to stand strong in your faith and overcome opposition. I speak that you will gracefully and gratefully receive help and graciously give others the help you can provide. I pray that you become prepared and empowered to successfully give birth to the various dreams housed within your spirit, without carrying your purposes amiss; while in-route to your destiny. I pray that as you journey through the pages of my heart, that these words will resuscitate your winded visions, invoke dormant or deferred dreams and speak life into the baby inside of you."*

Chapter Two

Conception Is Necessary Before Manifestation

Another phase for conception in the birthing process is the fertilization of an ovum, by a sperm; in order to form a zygote. Manifestation, on the other hand could be the embodiment of an intangible or variable thing. The title of this chapter reads, "Conception is necessary, before manifestation." Simply stated, you must first become pregnant, before you can ever give birth. So, how will we recognize or know when we have conceived?

From the moment of conception, an embryo constantly multiplies every cell within itself. This process is vital for every organ to properly develop for *internal growth*. It is important for us to understand this because everything that you think, say or do about pregnancy, either before the physical manifestation of a pregnancy and during the pregnancy has a profound effect on the unborn child.

The outcome of any pregnancy depends on many factors. The outcome here is also known as the manifestation. We have established the fact that pregnancy has huge emotional, mental, spiritual as well as physical components. Therefore, by understanding these truths, your pregnancy process may be a little easier and less problematic.

Overall, in the process of spiritual conception, GOD is yet at work. In ministry, conception represents the *"call."* It is the concept or notion that you are being led to do something bigger than yourself. You know that it is something divine because it is often associated with an immediate, eye opening realization. You then feel a tugging on the heart. Like the almost instant onset of nausea a woman feels in the first trimester. Later, a feeling of excitement ensues because you know that within you, something is growing. This embryo of purpose may come in the form of actual dreams, creative ideas or business strategies. It may even come in the simplistic form of intuition, but it is still proof that the concept now has life.

Ideas and Conceptions

An idea is any conception existing in the mind as a result of mental understanding, awareness, or activity. I prefer Webster's definition that states, *"an idea is a standard for perfection or a plan for action"*[8]. To be honest, I believe that every parent expecting a baby

---

[8] (*Merriam-Webster*, 2010).

believes that their baby will be perfect. *I know I believed it about mine, they were and still are!* I think the expecting parents have such high hopes and desires for their unborn despite the obstacles they know they'll face before leaving the womb and still, no one or anything can change their view. This is how we must be regarding our very own purpose. We must know that it is special, it is unique and perfect; a plan of action that only we can carry.

The mind is the broadest thing in this universe created by GOD; apart from the galaxy. Ideas *(truly good ones)* are conceived first in the mind, right? No, I will tell you that ideas, great and small come from GOD. I also believe that GOD equips each of us with a set of tools and gifts that will help the ideas that He gives us to grow and flourish. Just like the gynecologist who gives prenatal vitamins, performs series of tests and checks to further help the mother adequately care for her fetus. Although He truly knows us, GOD performs tests and checks to make sure that we will be prepared to serve as a viable sanctum for that which he plants within us.

Ideas rule the world. Think of some of the greatest ideas of our time. Who would have ever thought that the pony express would evolve into social media that hosts evolutionary platforms such as Facebook and Twitter? These platforms have even changed the way we do business from corporate America to the church. For example, in the ministry, we used to depend on someone showing up for service or giving a courtesy call or unexpected visit to witness. Now, we can go live and share the goodness of JESUS from the woods to the world; with a simple smartphone and internet connection.

I don't know if the inventors of these platforms knew and had a relationship with GOD The Father, and yet their ideas have changed the world. How much greater can you be, and change you can make for the good of mankind, when you have yoked your dreams and visions with the power of GOD? All you must do is ask! The Bible expresses that GOD *"...is able to do immeasurably more than all we ask or imagine, according to his power that is at work within us"*[9] (NIV).

GOD can give you these ideas if you ask Him. As a matter of fact, there is a great story in the Bible[10] that provides a great example of this concept. There was a man named Jacob. He worked for his uncle Laban, tending sheep. Jacob simply wasn't satisfied with just working for someone else. He knew that there was more purpose to his life than the position he was in at that moment. He desired freedom. It is amazing what can happen when you realize that your current position is only a temporary launching pad for your true purpose! Let that seep into your spirit right now. Make a declaration that where you are is not where you shall remain! Your purpose has a destiny and that destiny will be fulfilled, in JESUS' name! GOD's word is life!

Now back to Jacob and his situation. Jacob gets an idea that will enable him to become free. It is important to know that Jacob's name means supplanter, one who overthrows; undermine. So, if we simply look at Jacob's name, we can assume a couple of things about

---

[9] Ephesians 3:20 NIV
[10] Genesis 30: 27-34

him. First, Jacob must be a hard worker and not afraid to get his hands dirty. Second, we can suspect that Jacob possesses and innate ability to supplant something or someone. GOD had already pre-wired Jacob to be cunning, inquisitive, resilient and a carrier of wealth.

In short, Jacob worked for his uncle for 14 years. He was tired because he was overworked, underpaid and never appreciated. Yet, Laban profited greatly from Jacob being in his household. Jacob finally decided that he was fed up and he was going home. I must stop and ask you, the reader a question. Have you been in a place where you felt like GOD lead you, but you just did not fit in; that place where you seem to always stand out, even when you want to remain inconspicuous? Well, I have! I felt out of place, disconnected and I was sinking in disgust because I knew my purpose couldn't happen in that place. I have another confession, I was wrong! GOD deliberately put me in a place of discomfort and discontent to force the greatness in me to come out! Jacob experienced the same thing with his uncle Laban.

Now, Laban became very wealthy from Jacob's labor. So, you can imagine his level of anxiety and anguish when Jacob, his money maker, told him he was leaving. Well, like any greed driven and selfish person, Laban knew he could not allow that to happen. Laban had a deceitful heart and Jacob only wanted what he earned and to move on, but the word declares tha*t "GOD shall make your enemy your footstool."* This simply means that those people who have secretly discussed your downfall and demise will not only see you live, but GOD will expose them in shame. In addition, GOD will allow their heads to be the very stepping stone that you need to get closer to your purpose!

Jacob knew his uncle. He knew what moved and motivated him as well. Now the idea! Both Jacob and Laban had one. You must know this, in your carrying of purpose you will encounter problems, but you mustn't panic, don't be anxious! Within you, is the safest place for your purpose to reside. So, when Jacob went to Laban, Laban asked Jacob, *"how much do I owe you nephew?"* Remember Laban loves his money, so he isn't really moved to give Jacob anything. Yet, Laban knows that his association with Jacob is what has blessed his household. Laban underestimates Jacob's discernment. Jacob knows that Laban has changed toward him. Laban has already planned to use his wealth to entice Jacob to keep working for him. Jacob responded to his uncle's question in a way that secretly excited Laban. Jacob told Laban that he did not owe him anything. Imagine the dignified look of arrogance and triumph on Laban's face. He surely thought he had won.

You may blame it on Jacob's *cunning* skills, but GOD had already equipped Jacob to overcome this attempt to abort his purpose. Jacob and Laban made a shady deal, but it was very simple and precise. Jacob's plan, which was a bi-product of a talk he had with the Lord; begins to unfold.

Jacob tells Laban, according to Genesis 30:31-33, *"But if you will do this one thing for me, I will go on tending your flocks and watching over them: 32 Let me go through all your flocks today and remove from them every speckled or spotted sheep, every dark-colored lamb and every spotted or speckled goat. They will be my wages. 33 And my honesty will testify for me in the future, whenever you check on the wages you have paid me. Any goat in my possession that is not speckled or spotted, or any lamb that is not dark-colored, will be considered stolen"* (NIV).

Now, Laban was sure Jacob had lost his mind. Jacob took out the colored and spotted sheep and gave them to Laban, whose sons took them away a distance of three days' journey (verse 36). This left Jacob with only the pure white sheep. How was a white goat going to bring forth speckled goats? Laban quickly agreed to this deal! Many times, the enemy will have you backed in a corner thinking that he has won. Then GOD, like the amniotic fluid sac, envelopes us and our vision to prevent any attack that poses a risk to our developing baby!

When a woman sees that baby bump for the first time or feels the first flutter from the baby, I am sure she is filled with joy. It is exciting when we can see the evidence of our conception, even when we have yet to give birth. Remember, Jacob had the weaker cattle sent away and he vowed to tend to the strong sheep that remained. Jacob is still working for Laban, but as he does so, his purpose has time to mature, gain strength and fully develop.

Ultimately, Jacob finally out witted his uncle. Jacob used a method that was normal during this time, that helped animals go into heat. When an animal goes into heat, it means they are ready to begin conceiving. This method used by Jacob and divine intervention from

GOD allowed the white sheep to conceive and birth sheep that resembled the speckled sheep that Laban's sons took away. This miracle took place and Jacob became a wealthy man. Laban could not believe that he lost! He even tried to change the deal but could not.

Let this story of Jacob encourage you. You may be in a place where you feel stagnated, but GOD has already set a plan for your survival. When you trust GOD with your life anything and anyone attached to your life will be blessed too. A mother with-child cannot eat and the fetus doesn't eat too. If a mother is on drugs while she is carrying the baby, it is very likely that her baby will be born with an addiction to the very drugs given to it in the womb. Your purpose works the same way. Whatever you feed your mind; will have a major effect on your ideas, visions, dreams and purpose. Additionally, if we act hastily, we may slip and fall, and this may result in a miscarriage. Jacob was patient as he watched his purpose grow gracefully and with vigor; while Laban awaited his downfall.

Everything that Jacob endured in the conception stage, mattered in the outcome of his purpose. He trusted GOD with his life. He had faith similar to Job's. *"Though you slay me, yet will I trust you."* Though I don't have the privilege to physically birth a child, I do know that it is a tedious process. I know that the one with-child must go through some major transitions. One may have swollen feet; another may experience insomnia and difficulty getting comfortable enough to rest. Then others may endure more life-threatening instances such as elevated blood pressure or fetal distress. Regardless of the obstacle, a woman is resilient, and most are relentless in their efforts to protect their seed and give birth.

Jacob exemplified this same tenacity and when it was time, Jacob triumphed. When GOD drops an idea, or dream in the center of your purpose, do not ignore it. Use it to help what you have conceived to grow, so that your purpose is able to manifest; in due season.

If The Conception is of GOD, it will indeed Manifest!

If the conception is of GOD, the manifestation will occur. This works for all things spiritual and physical. Surely, you may have heard the question, "Where did you get your inspiration?" Most great inventors, artists in music, photography, sculpting or anyone who has done something significant, has probably been bombarded with this inquiry. What inspires people, drives the very essence of who they are and what comes from them. Inspiration is powerful. Inspiration is like a seed. Without a seed, no plant, human or animal would have existed. The same goes for anything that we do. Without inspiration, our dreams, ideas, plans or our purpose for that matter, would not happen. GOD's desire to be worshipped and praised were some of the inspirations for his creation of man. Though we failed him, His unrequited love, inspired Him to send His Son to save our sin-sick souls. If inspiration prompted GOD, and we are made in His image, then we too must be inspired in order to produce purposefully. Now, stop and think from where does your inspiration come? What motivates you to fulfill your GOD given purpose?

I am an observant person. In my observation of others, I have learned that people are motivated by many different things. Motivation is synonymous with inspiration in this analogy. I am sure that our ancestors that were subjected to the brutality and hardships of slavery were inspired to be free because of the liberty associated with it. I have even heard that coyotes are so eager to live, that they will bite off their own trapped foot; simply to escape death. Does anything inspire you enough to put your life on the line? Well, if not, you may want to re-evaluate your purpose. JESUS was so motivated to fulfill the perfect will of GOD that he died for you and me! Death may seem like an extreme, but many times in order for our purpose to come to fruition and live, we may have to let something within us, around us or attached to us die. In our walk with GOD, we must be inspired by His divine destiny so that purpose may flourish within us naturally and spiritually. GOD needs to be at the center of it all.

The bible instructs us to, "Let this mind be in you that was also in Christ JESUS" (KJV). I interpret this as saying that we must align our plans and GOD given purpose with GOD's will, timing, resources, etc. For if we do these things, then our inspiration is evident. GOD-inspired ideas are not always easy to come by, but through revelation from the Holy Spirit, we can catch a glimpse of GOD's plan. This immediately reminded me of my experience in a movie theater.

Whenever you go to watch a movie there are always previews shown before the feature film. When you watch the previews, it gives you an *idea, (there's that word again)* of what to expect from the film before you even get the opportunity to see the actual film. Previews have the power to inspire or invoke an onlooker to go see the movie or it may lose their interest altogether.

Let me give you another example. That pregnant mom that we have discussed in the last two chapters is now, in her second trimester. The best part about this trimester is two-fold, at least that's what I have heard. The first great thing is that their morning sickness usually leaves during this period. However, the most exciting thing is being able to get the ultrasound of the baby. I remember how excited I was to see a glimpse of what I had created on that little black and white paper. I couldn't share the joy of feeling a kick but seeing a snippet of what was coming was awe-inspiring.

Likewise, when we can preview the things that are within and come from our purpose, it ignites some and recharges others to keep persevering. Remember this, we don't just sit and wait for GOD to do the work, we work along with Him. This doesn't mean that GOD needs our help. No, it means that in waiting you are acting like the waitress or waiter in your favorite restaurant. You must sacrifice, serve, stand, sit, and do whatever is needed to accommodate the customer. In this case, the customer is GOD. Proverbs encourages us to *"trust in the Lord"* in all that we do and to refrain from *"leaning to our own understanding."* This means entrusting GOD with our ideas and allowing him to make it plain enough for us to carry it out. I can guarantee one thing, if He said it, He shall perform it! Trust the process!

A snapshot of my Manifested Process

I felt a tug on my heart early in life. This call spoke out to me when I was barely able to reason. Yet, I knew it was pushing me to be different. I began my spiritual walk with GOD prior to my teenage years and later heeded the call to preach the gospel; December of 1985, at the age of 18. I remember my mom and dad were singing with a gospel group called, *"The Happy Land Singers."* Boy, I would be so excited on Saturday nights, as I listened to them practice some of the old 100's they would be singing; come Sunday morning. I always anticipated Sunday because I knew that I would get to go with them to church. That was truly a time that I cherish, because in this day and time people don't seem to be as excited to go worship.

Nevertheless, a divine appointment took place that pushed purpose in me. When I accepted my calling, my father had recently became the pastor of Benford Chapel Baptist Church in Tenaha, Texas. As a matter of fact, my daddy is still laboring in ministry there. My father allowed me to become the youth pastor. GOD began to use me and Benford Chapel became the place to be for service. We had so many young people coming to serve the Lord.

In 1987, I moved to Seattle, Washington and united with the Rose Hill Baptist Church. I became an associate minister there. In 1988, I was elected as interim Pastor of St. Matthews Baptist Church, where I served for one year. It was there that I noticed how GOD was really working through me. During my stay in Seattle, I received the Holy Ghost. *That's when I saw my baby bump.* I had conceived the moment I accepted Christ, but I didn't realize my purpose was being nurtured all those years. I could feel the anointing, and I saw a fragment of GOD's planted purpose. I made many friends while there in the Emerald City. One night, I went to visit with Bishop Drake at his church. He laid hands on me and I felt the power of GOD like never before. Receiving the Holy Ghost changed my life tremendously.

In 1990, I moved back to Louisiana and became the Pastor of New Zion Baptist Church. GOD allowed me to do some awesome things in my home church. This was the church in which I was raised, by my grandfather. I was overwhelmed with emotion as I thought to myself, if my grandfather had lived longer, I would have been his Pastor. Me, pastoring was something he always spoke of. I served at New Zion for 10, great years, but I always felt that I wasn't doing enough. I needed to do more in the kingdom.

Union Spring Church was where I needed to be. So, I followed the leading of The Lord and began to serve here at Union Spring Church. I continue as Senior Pastor here for the past 23 years and counting. GOD has done and is still doing great things in this ministry. We have seen miracle after miracle happen. We are not a mega church, but we have a mega spirit. We have learned to work with what is in our hands and watch GOD give the increase.

In 2003, GOD gave me a vision to start Anointed Word Ministry, Inc. This ministry was envisioned and created as an entity to promote pastors and leaders who desired to go to the next level in ministry. July 2003 was our first "Word Explosion Conference." Not only did GOD show up, He showed out. This service led many ministries to join the Anointed Word movement. Many years had passed, since the last time I felt my own purpose had been miscarried. Through this vision, GOD had revived a dead situation.

As you may know, in any ministry or business, you will have those that are gung-ho for the vision GOD gives you, however, there will always be those that come to see what you're doing, only to become naysayers. Some stayed, some walked away, and some even tried to hurt us, but GOD has protected us! My advice to you, *"Never let anything hinder what GOD calls you to do."* That was the spirit I had. I refused to let those who were not privy to my vision, to deter me from doing that which I knew GOD had called me to do! I took on more responsibilities for the kingdom.

GOD saw fit to allow me to lead another flock, in conjunction with the church I already had. The First Baptist Church of Cedar Grove accepted me as their Pastor in 2012. Great things began to happen for this ministry as well. People were being blessed, relationships were created and the congregation grew immensely. As a matter of fact, it expanded so much that a new sanctuary is currently scheduled to be built soon.

In August of 2016, I was appointed as the as the State Bishop of Louisiana under Global United Fellowship. In 2018, I was officially consecrated to the Office of Bishop in The Lord's Church. This was one of the most humbling experiences in my ministry. Today, I believe that I am in my season of manifestation.

I have faith that the promises of GOD, for me are truly coming into fruition.

Things were not easy when I first stepped out on faith into the area of an establishmentarian. So, I admonish you, "If you are a serious visionary, searching for an idea for your next startup; *you may want to seek ways to motivate and inspire yourself*. Then, once you find that idea…

1. Write it down!
2. Plan it out!
3. Nurture it!
4. Pray over it!
5. Push it out!

Do not stop pressing until GOD births that thing right out of you! Habakkuk 2:2 says, "Write the vision and make it plain…" When He gives it to you, He will birth it through you!

It takes time to manifest

The issue of manifestation should be treated carefully. A lot of charismatic Christians make the mistake of seeking an *experience,* when they should be seeking manifestation. As Christians, where should we get our ideas? Where can we get our inspiration? The first place is in the Bible.

[11]The Bible says, *"The word of GOD is a lamp unto my feet, a light unto my path"* Read the Bible! It is imperative to the development of you, your purpose, your dreams, your goals and anything that you do in this life. Many believe that the Bible is outdated, and/or they question its validity. No matter how *outdated* anyone may think the Bible may be, I firmly believe the widely used acronym; that it is our "<u>B</u>asic <u>I</u>nstructions <u>B</u>efore <u>L</u>eaving <u>E</u>arth!"

Let me be really honest, reading the Bible does not only tell you about GOD. This book is a revelatory x-ray that reveals to you, who you are through the eyes of your Heavenly Father. It exposes you to the very nature of GOD, man and those enemies that we will encounter in this life. The Bible helps to give you insight into the mind of GOD. The Bible is an essential manual that will guide you, encourage you, convict you, enlighten you, give you peace and sustain you; as it is a direct connection to GOD's thoughts. [12]*"...The word of GOD is quick, and powerful, and sharper than any two-edged sword, piercing even to the dividing asunder of soul and spirit, and of the joints and marrow, and is a discerner of the thoughts and intents of the heart"*.

How can we use the bible in the process of carrying purpose? First, anything that we do for GOD is always associated with process. Because there is a process, conception to manifestation does not happen overnight. The Bible is like vitamins and supplements required during a pregnancy. When used, it will help

---

[11] Psalm 119:105 New International Version.
[12] Hebrews 4:12 King James Version

provide necessary nutrients and substantial nourishment essential for the maintenance and growth of life for you and the purpose your carrying. It also serves as a major source of inspiration and confirmation of GOD's promises throughout this what could be a long and painful, but vital process.

Now, that you know to use the bible to assist you, once you have conceived. What's next? You need to understand that GOD is there to see you through the process. You may begin a project that you know came directly from the mouth of GOD, but it just seems to not be working. Do you sometimes want to give up? Do you begin to question whether GOD even spoke to you? Yes, these are natural human feelings, when things that we believe in are not coming together the way we imagined or expected that they would, or in the time we thought. In other words, it is okay to have a momentary lapse in your faith. Yet, it is not beneficial to you or your vision to lose your faith and or abort the "baby" you're carrying.

I recall a time during my earlier years in ministry that really tested my faith. It seemed that everything that GOD was telling me to do; I would do, but it wouldn't work. I studied my word, I yoked myself with men and women of GOD that could encourage me, and nothing was working. One day I went to GOD and I said, *"Lord I know that you have told me to do all of these things. I know that I hear from you. I know that your word is true, but why is it not working?"* I clearly heard the voice of GOD say to me, *"I gave this to you, but now is not the time. Wait!"*

Often times, when we get a great idea it is so good that we want to get it done right then. That response that I received from GOD slapped me right in the face. *"Wait!"* I was a little upset, but I was more hurt because I had been doing so much to try and get all these things done to please GOD. Then, to hear that all He wanted was for me to stand still. I couldn't understand it, I was disappointed, I felt like I wasted time. So, I was led to the bible.

GOD took me to Genesis 6 and the story of Noah. It is a familiar story, but the gist of the story is simple. Noah was instructed, by GOD to build an ark. Well, during this time there had never been rain, but GOD told Noah to build a big boat because it was going to rain. Noah was 500 years old when he was told to build the boat. The crazy thing is he was 600 years old when he finished the project. Now, I was like, *"Lord I don't have 100 years to do all the things that you want me to do."* I still wasn't getting it.

So, during this 100-year span, Noah was given specific instructions on how to construct this massive ark. *"...This is how you are to build it: The ark is to be three hundred cubits long, fifty cubits wide and thirty cubits high. Make a roof for it, leaving below the roof an opening one-cubit high all around. Put a door in the side of the ark and make lower, middle and upper decks."*[13] Then, GOD said to me through this scripture, *"I have given you the idea, but you began before I had given you all of the instructions."* That word hit me hard!

---

[13] Input source scripture

After receiving the orders to build the ark *(the idea)*, I believe that Noah was probably like, *"GOD what is an ark? Rain? What is rain and how will this ark protect us from it?"*

Naturally, we as humans want to question things we don't know because it helps us many times to process new or crazy information and what next steps we should take. Yet, that is contrary to what GOD really desires of us. He wants us to trust in His ability to be GOD so, that we become confident that He will give every single detail to us and bring it all to pass according to His will. Philippians declares that, *"He that began a good work in you is faithful to perform it…"*[14].

Once Noah was given the specific details, he did not rush into it, remember it took 100 long years to finish. He took his time, so that he could ensure that he was building exactly what GOD ordered. He had to because his and his family's lives depended on it. The vital points that I want you to take from these personal experiences of mine are:

1. *Hear the idea, pray.*
2. *Wait for the instructions, pray.*
3. *Listen to all that GOD is instructing, pray.*
4. *Move when GOD says move, praying along the way.*

Consequently, I had not fully listened to the instructions of GOD once I heard the idea. That is why nothing was working to the level of excellence I knew GOD wanted. Also remember this, your

---

[14] Input source scripture ESV

life, the life of your family and others may be depending on your purpose being fulfilled. Therefore, do not risk miscarrying your purpose because you don't wait on GOD. The vision may tarry; which means it may take some time. Yet, the bible encourages us, that though there is a process, it shall come to pass.

I Heard GOD, Now What?

Sometimes, when we really believe that we are on the "right path" challenges won't come. Yet, the truth is, that's when they come the most. Your ability to wait upon the Lord while everything seems to be crumbling, facilitates the manifestation process. Hold to the course, stand firm and don't quiver. The Lord is with you and he will see you through! Although those things that I did, failed at first. I was able to go back and do them over, the way GOD wanted. Each venture was successful in its own way. Most importantly, I learned that hearing and listening are two different things. I also learned that when we listen and apply the word, GOD's instructions are clearer.

GOD could be revealing something to you right now but because of your crowded thoughts, being busy, or your doubt, you can't grasp all that GOD has in store for you. How many times have you thought of something and you desire to put it into action, but you discard it a few minutes later? You throw it out because you find it irrelevant or purposeless? When you get these special thoughts, take your time to think through them. Is it something realistic? Can you achieve this? Once you feel that strong feeling telling you that you can do it, quickly write it down. Note the date and don't hold back anything when you are writing. Feel free to pour out your mind on the pages of the book. After this, you have two options; act immediately or keep for future use. I would consider consulting GOD before I act, but if you are prompted to move quickly, do not delay!

If you believe in something, do it. Do not be deterred. You have GOD on your side and that's all it takes to make it to the finish line. If He said it, He will do it!

CHAPTER THREE

Pregnant With A Purpose

I remember being a young man who was very active in sports and other extracurricular activities. Still, I always found myself being drawn to being in service, with the Saints. Saints is another name for the people of GOD. Before I was called into the ministry, I recall being at a church with about seven or eight young men and my father brought us together and formed a male chorus. We called ourselves the "Faltine Male Chorus." We were all just teenagers and I really thank my father for bringing us together because it helped keep us as young men in the church and developed a familiarity with an acute aspect of my purpose to the church arena.

Being an encourager, being an exhorter of the faith.

This great opportunity as a young man gave me a snapshot of my future ministry. Then, I had to travel to minister at the age of around 18 and we decided to change our name to the Faithful Few

Male chorus. We would sing and GOD blessed us to go all over Texas and Louisiana to uplift and encourage GOD's people through song. Despite this, I realized that there was a greater call and a nagging urge for me to do more. It was in the winter months when my world shifted forever. It was in 1985, the Tuesday before Thanksgiving, right before the holidays. I received a call that my grandfather wasn't feeling well. As far as I knew, he had never really been sick or anything close to that. After getting that call, I just knew once I got to my grandfather, he would be okay.

I rushed from Keatchie, Louisiana to get to Grand Cane, Louisiana; which was only a few miles apart. I was rushing, because I was meeting other family members that had gone ahead of me to check on him. They were trying to get in the house and couldn't get in. Eventually one of my relatives had to break a window to get in the home to check on my grandfather. I arrived later to news that I never expected to hear. My grandfather was gone. This couldn't be real, but now I had to face the reality of continuing life without my hero. I must say that this news made my world crumble in ruins. My grandfather had transitioned and left me numb inside.

After a few days had passed, all I could reflect on was all the good my grandfather taught me. How he was a strong man of GOD and worked to help his family and the community. I had no idea of what GOD wanted me to do at the time. I just knew the man who helped raise me, who taught me about GOD, faith, family and serving GOD had left me. Now this is a moment of shock and I needed HELP! In my very young years I had to learn the difficult lesson that, *the Lord giveth and the Lord taketh away*[15]. It was my grandfather's time to return to His Father and reap his eternal reward. At first, I was upset but I had to accept the reality that he would not be back, and I needed to make sure I carried on his legacy of faith that he instilled in me! I understand that it takes time for some to get to this place of acceptance but with GOD's power you can. It wasn't easy but GOD showed me that no matter how upset we get with Him for allowing some of life's disappointments to happen; He still loves us and is always available to help us grow through it all.

When we find ourselves pulling away for whatever reason, GOD is patiently waiting on us to find our way back to Him. Even when we place most of our trust in external bodies or forces, GOD sits back, leaves us to wander in the wilderness of self-struggle until we get back to him.

Now, how did I move forward and still embrace the future without my "Paw-paw"? I didn't know how to at first, but I quickly learned through my grandfather's death. After burying my grandfather, the Saturday after Thanksgiving I had an epiphany. It was a call to action, I couldn't totally explain it, but I just knew it was time. So, after the funeral on Saturday all my family planned to stay at home. I was beckoned by the Holy Spirit to attend church the following morning. So, I went to church and that Sunday was like no other Sunday before, because the Holy Spirit confirmed within

---

[15] Input source scripture

my spirit why I was there. I was sanctioned by the Holy Spirit to announce my call into ministry.

I was only 17 years old, but when ministry calls its time to go. GOD had plans for me and they were good[16], I just had to get started. The church celebrated it and was as excited as me. I had only wished my grandfather had the opportunity to be here to witness this monumental milestone in my life. Quickly after service, I ran home, and I shared the news with all my family members. They were excited to hear the news, everyone celebrated with me. I was greeted with lots of love, hugs and kisses, my parents were very proud. I had a feeling in that moment that everything was going to be alright. This spiritual decision shifted the trajectory of my life forever and even though I was still hurt about the absence of my grandfather there was a greater spiritual force that was giving me strength and purpose to move forward.

This experience reminded me of the story of Isaiah[17]. It may me think to myself… Why did GOD prepare Isaiah in the same year that King Uzziah died? Well, I believe GOD is always working according to His own plan and not ours. There was a lot of activity going on around me and a roller coaster of emotions ensued. While in my pain, GOD was calling me forth. GOD is just good like that. Even as He was in pain from watching His children constantly sin against him, He still sent JESUS to die for us.

---

[16] Insert source scripture
[17] (Isaiah 6:1-8).

Now, I was pregnant with purpose! I'm a witness that in your pain GOD will speak and give you an opportunity to prove that He can use you to bring forth new life; even when life has been taken away from you. This is the whole message and purpose of Christ. To teach us that, when we are in Him, we become new and burying the old man gives us new life!

Experiencing the death of a loved one in my life taught me that sometimes death can push you to focus on getting your own personal life in order. It causes you to remember that you're going to also die one day. The death of one of my heroes now left me more postured with a greater desire to live a more meaningful life of purpose. This is when I became aware that I was pregnant with purpose and I was ready to prepare myself to manifest everything GOD predestined me to do. My spirit was full of excitement because GOD had chosen me to carry his word and deliver it to his people. What an honor!

Purpose could pop up on us at any time! For example, think about meeting the person that will be your spouse. You could meet them anywhere and at any time. If you're married think about it. Were you expecting to meet that special person when and where you encountered them? When that opportunity comes you feel butterflies and you're floating on cloud nine. There is no greater feeling in the world to you at that moment. The same happens when we are pregnant with GOD's purpose.

I'm going to have a baby

There is no news as joyful and exciting as finding out you are having a baby. In some cases, the news isn't as great, but when the baby comes, all that changes. What does the Bible have to say about children? Psalm 127:3-4 tells us, *"Happy and Blessed, and fortunate is the man whose quivers is filled with children."* The point here is that we should always be happy to have children. For some, the joy of a marriage is fully achieved when the wife is pregnant, and the family welcomes a child. Two become three. And three is a crowd. The feelings of excitement cannot be isolated from every human emotion, but something becomes paramount here. Being pregnant is not the only stage, nursing the child in the womb and having a safe delivery is also as important as the ovulation process. Yes, we may be excited, but our happiness is laced with nervousness. Remember, in our journey being pregnant, really means carrying purpose. It is important to understand that our gifts, talents or that business, is what GOD has entrusted into our hands.

Understanding The Call

It is very possible to have a vision and lack proper understanding of what that vision entails. *(Remember my prior confession and the story of Noah.)* Coming to the knowledge of what 'your purpose' entails could be scary. Let's recall the little boy in Chapter 1 that wanted to be a pastor, however wanted nothing to do with funerals? He had little to no understanding of the pastoral vision, but he understood that he was fearful of funerals.

Understanding your vision unlocks all the available resources needed for you to achieve it. And this is where help comes in. You don't only need help to understand your vision; you need it to unlock your potential.

First and foremost, we have received "the call" as Christians to servant ministry. Most of the time when we hear the word "ministry", what comes to mind is pastoring. Ministry isn't just for a pastor, but ministry is for every believer. It is very important that we really take time to find out what the Bible says about "ministry". The scriptures places great emphasis on "Ministry." What is ministry? Ministry is a call to serve others and not necessarily a call to hold a position of authority for others to just serve us. JESUS said in Mark 10:43, *"Whoever desires to be great among you must be your servant."* According to Merriam Webster, The Greek word *diakonov* translates from diako which means: *to run errands. One who does the commands of another, especially from a* master. Who then, is our master? JESUS Christ! He is Lord[18].

So those of us who are pregnant with purpose are called to serve. In fact, every believer is pregnant with purpose and has an obligation to operate in ministry. So even if you are starting a business, you should operate from a place of love and humanitarian servitude. See ministry is an avenue that ultimately enables us to share the love of Christ in what we do.

---

[18] Input source scripture

When we operate from a place of love, we win souls for Christ. Therefore, JESUS said, *"That if I be lifted up, I will draw all men/women unto me."*[19] So, if love (GOD – For GOD is love) be lifted, He will draw men and women unto Himself. Thus, we have a mandate, a spiritual baby in our womb. The pregnancy did not just get there. We are pregnant with GOD's purpose. With this purpose, we must avoid the dangers that may try to come to abort our baby.

Ministry, Gifting, Business

Some are pregnant with a single child, or twins, or even triplets, etc. In the same way, spiritually, GOD could impregnate us with different things at the same time. Business ideas, Gifts and classical Ministry are just a few. Sometimes these callings can intertwine to serve an overall greater purpose. But again, when we get the news that we are going to have a baby, the excitement comes in. When a lady is pregnant, she becomes giddy with excitement and who wouldn't be? Then, the giddiness dies down as soon as the pregnancy symptoms set in.

This is exactly what happens when we are pregnant with GOD's purpose, we become giddy and excited. Then, we can become overwhelmed with the demands and weight of the process, we get tired or discouraged. Now, we can also become zealous and find ourselves doing more than what we can really handle or get

---

[19] Input source scripture

burned out for lack of pacing ourselves. When a pregnant woman gets this way, she must seek out medical help.

When we are pregnant with purpose, whether it may be starting a new ministry or business, we should seek to find a mentor that can help us through the process of achieving our goals. These mentors can help give us the insight and proper nutrients we need to protect the growth and development of our baby. GOD has good thoughts towards us[20]. He knows that we need help and he is ready to provide us with the help we need. Having a mentor in our life and being open to their guidance is very important. We help ourselves when we are open to receiving direction and constructive criticism from our mentors. In the Bible Moses mentored Joshua, who later successfully helped the children of Israel get to their promise land. There are mentors who GOD will send in your life to help you get from one phase to the next. Learn to trust the process and know that all things are working together for your good!

Patience & Purpose

GOD shows us part of his plans, gives us instruction and then we should run off to complete the rest. Be careful! Sometimes the symptoms from carrying purpose may cause us to become short tempered with others and irritable when others are not doing what GOD has called them to do. Similar to the pregnant wife, who may get upset because her husband brought back the wrong type of

---

[20] Jeremiah 29:11-13

milkshake, but he was willing to go get it at 10 p.m. We cannot begin to doubt the purpose of GOD in others and find fault in what they are doing. We are to still go through our process and be patient with others, even when they get it wrong or don't listen.

Our life centers on GOD's purpose and the purpose surrounds us as a believer. The purpose here is the pregnancy. What GOD has placed in us as a gift, not a job we feel is necessary or needed for edification of the body of Christ. The only way we can edify the body of Christ without doing the opposite, is when we call on GOD for Help. From the start to the end, we need His help to avoid a miscarriage. Before you think of showing others their purpose, you should know yours. You can't give what you don't have. The purpose of GOD is much more important than we could ever imagine.

The purpose of GOD is much more important than anything in this world.

"The purpose of your life is far greater than your own personal fulfilment, your peace of mind, or even your happiness. It is far greater than your family, your career, or even your wildest dreams and ambitions. If you want to know why you were placed on this planet, you must begin with GOD. You were born by His purpose and for His purpose." -Rick Warren

5 Key Elements GOD Purposed for Us

1. To come to know The Lord and worship Him

Romans 6:12 (amp) insert

2. Love one another

We should enjoy the fellowship with other believers. We should seek to empower and encourage one another, as well as ourselves.

"I give you a new commandment: that you should love one another. Just as I have loved you, so you too should love one another."
John 13: 34-35 (*Amplified Version*)

3. Grow spiritually

He wants us to become more like His son JESUS Christ. This is what we know as Discipleship, being a disciple of JESUS Christ.

"May you abound in and be filled with the fruits of righteousness (of right standing with GOD and right doing) which come through JESUS Christ (the Anointed One), to the honor and praise of GOD [that His glory may be both manifested and recognized."
Philippians 1:11 (*Amplified Version*)

4. GOD's purpose for our lives is to serve others. We should be in Ministry to serve.

"As each of you has received a gift (a particular spiritual talent, a gracious divine endowment), employ it for one another as [befits] good trustees of GOD's many-sided grace [faithful] stewards of the extremely diverse powers and gifts granted to Christians by unmerited favor]. Whoever speaks, [let him do it as one who utters] oracles of GOD; whoever render service, [let him do it] as with the strength which GOD furnishes abundantly, so that in all things GOD may be

glorified through JESUS Christ (the Messiah). To Him be the glory and dominion forever and ever (through endless ages). Amen (so be it.)
1 Peter 4:10 (*Amplified Version*)

The ministry here encompasses all of who we are, what we are and what GOD wants us to be. The above Bible passage defines a spiritual talent, as a gracious divine endowment; a gift; a treasure GOD placed in us. Not for our own use but to bless the life of others. It goes further to describe how we should use our gifts. We should do all things with the strength GOD provides and for the glory of GOD.

5. Witness to others about GOD not for your sake but for His glory.

"For all [these] things are [taking place] for your sake, so that the more grace (divine favor and spiritual blessing) extends to more and more people and multiplies through the many, the more thanksgiving may increase [and rebound] to the glory of GOD."
2nd Corinthians 4:15 (*Amplified Bible*)

All of these and more are GOD's purposes for your life. So, before you get too excited, you should know that you can't afford to have a miscarriage. This is the part of the growth stage in conception that mental, physical, spiritual and public awareness are developed in the baby. Be advised that nothing in this stage is done on your own account or power. You received help.

CHAPTER FOUR

Someone(GOD) Partnered With Me To Form This Baby!

We have established that we all need help. When a lady gets pregnant, two people are responsible for that pregnancy. Her and the partner. When GOD places His purpose in our lives, He becomes responsible for helping us through that pregnancy. Just as a father claims responsibility over a child on earth and may be declined by the mother; we may find ourselves, rejecting GOD's help in fulfilling our life's purpose. I have found this one thing very important throughout my entire walk with GOD. He desires a firm relationship with us as believers. GOD wants us to believe Him for the tiniest things in our daily lives. Most of the time, when I misplace something, I would find myself asking GOD for help. Before I knew it, GOD would lead me exactly to what I lost.

I even started asking GOD to help me find a close parking spot, before I went to the grocery store. This was a simple case study of faith; I wanted to just see if GOD heard my request. Well, can I testify? After this request, I arrived at the grocery store and Yes! GOD did it! As soon as I pulled into the parking lot, a car was backing up right in the front of the store. See, we must get in the habit of asking GOD for help even in the smallest situations.

A healthy Bond with my Partner (GOD) helps me and my baby Thrive

Because it is GOD who gives us the instructions; we need to develop in every area of our lives. Sometimes it is easy to get caught up with the perks, fame, fortune and benefits that sometimes come with the type of purpose we carry as preachers. However, it is pertinent that we never forget who partnered with us; so that we could have the opportunity to carry purpose. Therefore, it is beneficial for all of us to stay connected to our partner (GOD). If we don't maintain focus, we can miss out on nutritional opportunities that can bring about a healthier baby, (vision) when it's time to deliver.

Now during this pregnancy, we can allow our ego to convince us that everything is all about us! This is how we can sometimes get distracted in life and believe that everyone should cater to us because we are pregnant. We must never forget that this opportunity to carry purpose is a gift to us from GOD, not just for us alone but to benefit the world. I believe that when we nurture our relationship with GOD, we can: 1. Develop a healthy mindset for life 2. Bring forth our baby. 3. We can embrace a balanced lifestyle of maturity in love, service and commitment. These 3 elements are needed to grow a healthy (baby) purpose.

Eating For Two

When a woman finds out that she is pregnant she is no longer just thinking about herself. She is put in a position where her baby's health is dependent on hers. So, when you become aware that you are pregnant with purpose your thought process must change. You can no longer think about how life can just work only for you. You are forced to figure out how life can work for you and your (baby) purpose.

If you are pregnant with a vision to start a new business, you can no longer just think about yourself. The purpose you are carrying, forces you to think about obtaining the right essentials that your business will need to succeed. You may be pregnant with a vision to go back to school and get your degree. The purpose in you now forces you to also think about the right prerequisites you are going to need in order to qualify to get into the school of your choice. You may be pregnant with a vision to develop a ministry program to help the youth in your community. This purpose forces one to think about the critical needs of those youth and how they can provide solutions that will offer them greater success.

Now to the Pastor, who has been called to launch a new church; the purpose in you forces you to think about how you can get a rhema word for the hundreds and thousands of people you will minister to.

We must believe that the purpose GOD has placed inside of us is a privilege and with His help, we are more than capable of carrying it to its completion. It goes beyond the confinements of ourselves, our reach and our limited views. When we allow GOD to partner with us throughout this spiritual pregnancy, we can witness how He can allow our purpose to transcend our greatest expectations. This should encourage us to maintain our partnership with GOD and allow Him to order our steps.

When we consistently nurture our relationship with GOD, we increase our chances of having a successful pregnancy. Having the daily assistance from our partner, decreases our mental and physical stress level. Taking time to pray and meditate on GOD's word can give us the energy and nutrition that we will need to help keep our baby growing healthy each day. Also, being connected with our partner in a healthy relationship gives us greater confidence to carry the vision on to its completion. Yes, it can be very intimidating at times to start something new and to accomplish something that you have never done before. But with GOD, you can rest assure that all things are possible if you only believe.

Making decisions in life that exclude our partner (GOD), causes us to develop an inconsistent relationship with Him, this increases our chances of having a miscarriage. I know sometimes in life we can get distracted and begin to put more of our focus on the excitement of preparing to have that new "baby" (business or position of authority in life); instead of maintaining our focus on the priority of bonding with our partner (GOD). There are promises that comes with being consistently connected to GOD and it isn't worth losing nor putting our purpose in threat of a miscarriage by operating in the alternative.

It is crucial that we protect our unborn purpose. Allow GOD to walk through the good, bad and the ugly moments with us. We will overcome every obstacle we face with our heavenly partner, instead of facing our problems alone. GOD promised that, *"He would never leave us nor forsake us, He would be there until the end of the world." Also, He promised that he would supply all of our needs according to his riches in Glory."*[21] So why wouldn't we want to be partnered with such and amazing GOD? *The blessings of the Lord maketh rich and addeth no sorrow*[22]. Having his partnership gives us a guarantee of unlimited success.

GOD is *my Business Partner*

Your baby isn't yours and yours alone, it is GOD's too. Remember, GOD partnered with you to have this baby. He deposited the business ideas in you. The Lord is the best business partner in the world. Why? Because He owns everything! "The silver is mine and the gold is mine, says the Lord of hosts."[23] What happens when you make the World Bank your Bank, with easy loans and zero

---

[21] Insert source scripture
[22] Input scripture source
[23] Haggai 2:8 (*Amplified Bible*)

collateral? Easy business, right? Well, we have more than just silver and gold. *"Both riches and honor come from you, and You reign over all. In your hands are power and might; in your hands it is to make great and give strength to all."*[24] We may think that this is not important, but I tell you it is. Business is not just about providing a service for others. It is also about making money to help sustain the business, so that services can continue. According to the world of business, if we are in business and not making money to sustain that business, that is considered a failed business.

In the past 20 years, I have owned and operated multiple businesses that have thrived and some that have dried up and withered away. What I had to learn as a business professional was that I wasn't in this by myself.

Catch Your Breath

When I was younger, I attempted to run my businesses, but I tried to do too much at one time. I had to learn how to pace myself overtime and understand that just as the weather has seasons, business has seasons too. I had to learn how to operate my businesses with a strategic success plan in place. There were so many resources available to me, but I had to learn where to get them and how to apply them to my business model. For the business owners who are struggling and trying to keep the doors open; ask GOD to help you and be prepared for any instructions He may give you. GOD has allowed me to cross paths with many great leaders

---

[24] 1 Chronicles 29: 12 (*Amplified Bible*)

and mentors that have taken me up under their wings. They helped me improve in the weaker areas of my business development.

I can remember one time that I called on GOD for help regarding my business... I had a landscaper company for many years that was very successful, but it wore me out. I was doing everything myself. I mowed the lawns, handled all the business and paperwork required, payroll, maintenance and the list goes on! A wealthy man said to me, **"Work smart and not hard!"** At that very moment, I realized that I could not do it all. I took his advice. First, I hired better employees. Next, I surrounded myself with people who had a mindset for business. Because I heeded the advice of someone who knew the business, the business has grown tremendously. Now, I work smart and not hard.

Another lesson I've learned as a business owner is this, I am only as strong my foundation, which starts with my team. I had to get a strong team of people to help me. The worst thing a business leader can do is to try to do everything by him/herself. It will be a disaster waiting to happen; especially if the services that your business offers needs more man power to succeed.

Business * Money * Faith

So, did you know that your view of money could predict how you see GOD? Billy Graham once said, *"If a person gets his attitude towards money straight, it will help straighten out almost every other area of his life. Tell me what you think about money, and I can tell you what you think about GOD, for these two are closely related.*

A man's heart is closer to his wallet than almost anything else." GOD owns your life, He owns your finances, He owns every business idea and He owns you. What else do you need? Why shouldn't you partner with Him?

Knowing the above should assure you that GOD is in control and He is a GOD of all possibilities. In my many years as a minister, I have come across a lot of people who are pregnant, but they don't want to deliver; they want to keep carrying. Now, I have never been a woman, but I am sure that carrying a child nine months is more than enough time for the women that do it. I have heard women firsthand complain about the wiles and woes of being pregnant. Why would anyone want to delay the delivery? Times have changed so much so, women can schedule the day that they want their babies to be born; if it is in the doctor's given timeframe.

In the animal kingdom there are instances where the animals carry the babies for a very long period. According to livescience.com, Elephants have a gestation period of about 645 days. Now I am no scientist, but I can count. A woman is pregnant around 280 days; which is 40 weeks. So, this means that an elephant is pregnant up to 95 weeks. That is amazing and scary all at once. I pose this question; how can your purpose grow within you once it has reached capacity?

Sometimes these kinds of people are the ones who become scared because they are pregnant. They get a small picture of GOD's plan and they retreat behind the wall of human reasoning. I am not exempted here. Think of all the questions a young mother may ask if she is having a baby alone. She may ask herself questions such as: How will I provide for a baby? I wonder if this will hurt. Will I be a good mother? Human inquisition could get in the way of GOD's purpose for us, if we allow it to do so. What happens is that we fail to remember that GOD has no human limitation?

GOD consoles us when He said that *"His power is made perfect in our weakness."*[25] Therefore, connecting our weakness to GOD thereby connects us to His strength, which makes us strong. We are equipped to carry purpose and that is why GOD has chosen us to be the vessels to do so. He called us to do what is impossible, in eyes of many. Despite their doubt, partnering with the Lord makes it possible. You know why? We have access! You and I can draw from the never ending well of His power and walk in unlimited success. GOD wants to remind us that He is in control and His power shines through our limitations. He wants us to live our best life without the fear of failing! Again, we are guaranteed to succeed when we walk in obedience to GOD.

GOD is work behind the scenes of our lives, He is in control.

What Christ expects from us is to remain in him.

"I am the Vine; you are the branches, whoever lives in Me and I in him bears much (abundant) fruit. However, apart from Me [cut off from the vital union with Me] you can do nothing"[26]

---

[25] 2 Corinthians 12:9
[26] John 15:5 (Amplified Bible)

You live in Christ and Christ lives in you. That is why the Bible passage above says that "a*part from me you are [cut off from the vital union]."* Obviously, there is a vital union between you and Christ. Your life becomes a reflection of Christ and Christ's light shines bright through you.

> *"I have been crucified with Christ [in Him I have shared His crucifixion]: it is no longer I who live, but Christ (the Messiah) lives in me; and the life I now live in the body I live by faith in (by adherence to and reliance on and complete trust in) the Son of GOD, Who loved me and gave Himself up for me."*[27]

We must have heard this a thousand and one times, especially when we surrendered our life to JESUS but fail to allow GOD's provision to work in us. Sometimes we come to a place in our Christian relationship when we fail to recognize that GOD is still with us. During this time of doubt, it is hard to believe that He hasn't gone and abandoned us. We begin to act on our own accord we push GOD away. Paul told the Galatians that *"...I live by faith (by adherence to and reliance on and complete trust in) the son of GOD..."* Do we really live by faith; total reliance on the Son of GOD? That is what GOD wants, total reliance and complete trust. GOD's presence and work in our life is bringing forth a higher purpose than we will ever know.

---

[27] Galatians 2:20 (Amplified Bible)

The ever-consistent presence of GOD is the most practical part of our life and ministry.

Look through the Bible. GOD keeps interfering with what we know as our *'personal business.'* He provided manna, quail and water for the children of Israel[28], He has been helpful. Is that not practical enough? In fact, the many stories about how GOD helped the children of Israel in the wilderness survive and conquer many challenges showcased His love for humanity. In the New Testament, JESUS fed the five thousand. He was being practical; while teaching those who followed him that they would be taken care of when they pursue GOD. The New Testament is full of practical teachings for Christian living. The GOD in the scriptures is exactly who we can expect GOD to be; real, practical and reliable. Most of the time, we allot a part of our lives to GOD. We limit the limitless GOD. Then we call on Him whenever we hit rock bottom. Just the exact opposite of what is present in the Bible. We really need to see GOD as our partner, our physical partner and spiritual friend. Did I just say a physical partner? Yes, I did. You should begin to work and walk with GOD so close that you see His hands in everything physical around you.

As Christians, we should learn to make our relationship with GOD so firm that we begin to see His hands literally in things around us. There was a man from Africa. He was a Christian. He had an amazing account of his own personal experience with this. I was dumbfounded by his story. According to him, he and his wife were

---

[28] Exodus 16 - New International Version

eating at the dining table. After blessing GOD for the meal, they started eating their breakfast by taking pieces of sliced bread. He took the first piece, his wife took the second, he took the third, and his wife took the fourth. Then he noticed that the bread had reduced drastically. He stared at his wife. *"It is not me, I just had my second slice"* his wife answered. Then he heard from GOD. *"Son, didn't you say, "I should eat with you, when you were praying?"*

Sometimes some people say to me, *"GOD's Purpose is not practical for today"* Well, I have this to tell you: GOD is an extreme realist. He wouldn't tell us what we can't do. This reminds me of one of JESUS' admonishments to be perfect[29]. I hear a lot of Christians say that it is not possible to be perfect but here is the response I give them; GOD said we should be perfect, not strive to be perfect. We can be perfect because our perfection is in GOD. He is the same yesterday, today and forever. If He says that we should be perfect, then we can be perfect.

I AM ATTRACTIVE & QUALIFIED TO DO THIS

Have you ever for once doubted the promises of GOD for your life? Have you ever for once experienced a crisis of belief? It can happen after GOD reveals his purpose to us. We must face it. Every Christian has or had fears they must face. When GOD finally reveals what He wants to do through you, you might meet a crisis of belief. What you do if this happens, determines several things. First, it determines how firm your relationship with GOD is and would be.

---

[29] Matthew 5:48

At one point in time in our church, our finance committee had told me, "Pastor, I can recall how many times you have taught us to walk by faith in every area in our life but is church budget an exception?" I was marveled at the question and I knew immediately that something wasn't right. The head of the finance committee continued. "Our budget is drafted out on the foundation of what we believe GOD can do. It doesn't show that we expect GOD to do anything."

Right there, I didn't have an answer and for the first time. I knew that he was right. You should know that you are attractive and qualified to be what you are called to in Christ. GOD placed this purpose in you. And He knows you are qualified to do this. Believe Him. Trust is judgement.

Just as I have mentioned, how we react to the crisis of belief determines how strong our faith would be or how weak it might appear. When we look at the redemptive work Christ has done for us, we find GRACE at the center of it all. Grace is unmerited favor. We don't deserve it, but GOD gave it to us anyway. Sending His Son to die for our sins is also the larger part of His grace showcasing itself in action. When we say we are qualified to fulfil GOD's purpose, we are not saying that because we are within ourselves; but because His grace has made us to be. *Having gifts (faculties, talents, qualities) that differ according to the* GRACE *given us!*[30]

Grace, like any other gift is free and is a part of GOD's character. Most times, we speak of grace as a commodity distributed and it is. It is a perfect description of GOD's character. GOD is a GOD of grace, He presents gifts to all men. He orchestrated the salvation process to prove His love for us. The grace of GOD is more than just GOD's help. It is GOD Himself.

Have you ever had an experience in life where you needed GOD to move on your behalf quickly? If GOD didn't move you would be without a roof over your head, or even dead! Well, I know how well GOD can show up and show grace to us even though sometimes we can't show up for ourselves or those we love or they for us.

I had been invited to preach a week-long revival in Canada for my friend Pastor Jackson. Closing that Friday night, I stated, "We must praise GOD no matter what. If the Lord takes everything we have, we should still have a reason to praise the Lord." Then I stated, "Lord if you take everything away from me, I will still praise you!" Well little did I know that those words would soon test my actions a few hours later.

I flew home Saturday morning. My wife was waiting for me at the airport. As we traveled home, we got a phone call that our

---

[30] Romans 12:6

house was on fire. By the time we got there, we had lost everything we owned. My wife, Michelle, thought the children had been burned alive in the fire but her sister had picked them up earlier that day. As I stood there looking at the ashes of everything I once owned, tears began to flow. Family members dropped by with their condolences. I stood there silently in disbelief. Michelle asked,

"What are we gonna do"? All I could say was, "I don't know".

We went to Wal-Mart to buy clothing for her and the boys to wear to church. That Sunday morning GOD reminded me of what I said on Friday. I began to praise GOD like never before because I said I would no matter what. We stayed in a hotel until a family member let us stay at their place. We went from pillar to post, but GOD!

We survived it all and I knew it was a temporary process we were going through. The devil tried everything to stop me from giving birth. I couldn't stop now. I had already conceived something so great and mighty. I had to push through all the pain. I lost all I owned besides what I came off the plane with, but GOD gave us back double for our trouble. I believed GOD could, I knew GOD would and GOD did it for us! I share this personal testimony to help someone who may be in the same situation now and feel like you are not going to survive all that you are going through. I am a witness that you were built to handle the pressure and what GOD brings you to, GOD will bring you through if you just keep going!

Now talking about a test of faith, this was a very difficult test! This wasn't something that only I had to go through, but my entire family had to go through this test. The human side of me was distraught for days but in my heart, I believed that GOD was extending grace to me and my family to showcase our faith, praise, love and belief. I cannot say this was easy because it was far from easy but when I put my focus on what really mattered, it was worship for me. I had to lay prostrate before the Lord and worship in a spirit of gratefulness because without GOD's grace, my wife and I could have had to plan a funeral for our children in addition, instead of just returning to a burned down house. But GOD's grace was at work!

My dear sister and brother in Christ, we must learn to pause for a moment, during those times of distress and adversity. We may be overwhelmed with emotions of disappointment, but we must work to align our focus to the GOD that is able. The GOD, who is the Potter who can take us, the clay and mold our lives into better than what we ever dreamed. The GOD that is able to keep us from falling. The GOD who supplies all our needs according to his riches in glory.

Now even though I had GOD, my faith, GOD's grace, my family and my mind; the enemy still tried to make me doubt my victory. See, when the pressure of trials starts to weigh us down, that is the best time to worship. In worship JESUS relieves our burdens and intercedes on our behalf to GOD the Father. This is the moment where you learn to pour out your heart and cry out to GOD. Then take time to just quiet your spirit and listen for GOD's love to speak life back into you. Worship is where your relationship with GOD is strengthened and Praising GOD brings about a release.

According to his grace, he has given us gift, talents, qualities and faculties. This grace makes us qualified, it makes us ready to accept the ministry which Christ has placed in our hands. Grace is not the only thing which qualifies us. As much as GOD wants to walk beside us to reach the Promised Land, He wants us to be rest assured that He is with us. That is why he made all the qualifications for handling His purpose or ministry, free.

Just as salvation is free, GOD placed all that we needed to fulfill His purpose in us, for free. Then He placed us, right in the center of His Grace.

CHAPTER FIVE

"Help Developing The Baby"

There are three stages of development of the fetus; the germinal, embryonic and the fetal stage. The fundamental thing to know is that development begins at conception and will not stop until when we leave the surface of the earth. We have established the fact that the knowledge of conception is coming into the understanding that we are pregnant with a purpose and that we need to nurture that dream (the conception). Having said that, there are three stages of pregnancy I do want to deal with, which are the three trimesters.

The first stage starts from the 1st week to the 14th week. During this stage, there is no obvious dramatic change existing in the woman's body. This could be likened to the conception stage. You have a purpose, you are pregnant. Yes! Glory to GOD! But we can't really see anything showing that you are truly pregnant. Through we may not be able to see any sign in you that you have evidence of purpose; that doesn't mean it doesn't exist. It's like having a business idea-your conception. It can grow to become big and bigger than what you think but you haven't taken any step. Or you are too afraid to take a step.

From the early stage of conception till death, the human body needs to be sustained. Food provides us with the right nutrients to live. Eating a proper nutritious diet offers numerous health benefits that keep you mentally and physically well. Following a healthy diet reduces the risk of having chronic diseases, such as diabetes, heart disease and cancer. A balanced diet provides the energy needed, to keep active throughout the day. It also gives you the nutrients needed for growth and repair. Eating the right foods and feeding our bodies with the right nutrients, gives us strong bones and teeth, provides a perfect healthy heart diet and maintains a healthy weight. The benefits of having the right nutrients in the body cannot be overemphasized. We help ourselves with the right food and sometimes we may need the help of a nutritionist when it comes to special diets. The same works for spiritual food, you eat the right food and fill yourself with the perfect spiritual nutrient. You can also have a spiritual nutritionist when it comes to having a special diet.

The Second Trimester

In addition to the first stage, we have the second, which is the simplest stage of all. It lasts until the seventh month of pregnancy. Most of the symptoms experienced in the first stage subsides or actually goes away completely. Nevertheless, other symptoms begin to set in like shortness of breath, sensitivity in breast, dizziness, pain and muscle ache. In this stage, the baby continues to **grow**. The child begins to blink, kick and move inside the uterus. According to experts, women should increase the **intake of calcium** this time to aid the growth of the baby's skeleton system. Nutrition is a pivotal and fundamental part throughout the pregnancy stages. It's important to take serious cognizance of what to eat during this stage.

The Importance of Nutrition After Conception

Don't be satisfied with just having a good idea. Feed it, nurture it, and build upon it until it becomes too large for you to hide it and your pregnant stomach bulges out. When it comes to the business world, we can increase ideas by coming up with a great idea also. How can you get more ideas? Simple! Feed your idea. Picture your ideas like atoms floating around. You know how it happens in the old chemistry movies. Atoms float around and collide to form a big bang! *(A chemical reaction)* Something new is created. Something either exploded or maybe it all fizzled out. This happens to ideas too. It takes place inside your brain. Here, atoms are not floating all around, but pieces of information and other ideas are. They could occasionally bump into each other. Then what happens? A new idea emerges. Reading has been one of the oldest and best ways to feed your idea. Get books about your idea, if you can't find one. Break your idea into small chunks and find books about each chunk. The most surprising thing about knowledge is that there isn't a lot of untouched brand-new knowledge. This may come as a surprise to you. Your multi-million-dollar idea could be what someone, somewhere just presented as a proposal. Execution is what matters. Our ideas could only be fed properly when we ask for help.

Feeding The Spiritual Man

There is need for us to participate with GOD in the development of our spiritual growth. Our spiritual life shouldn't be stagnant, and, in this chapter, I pray the Lord opens your eyes to see the help you need from within. So, when it comes to spiritual growth you will be ready to receive the necessary tools and instructions that will help you achieve a better spiritual life.

When it comes to spiritual growth, we should take note of the following things:

- Expectancy
- Reverence
- Alertness
- Obedience to GOD

Let's take a deeper look into these elements that will help our spirit grow healthier each day.

- **Expectancy**: When you come to the throne of grace (approaching GOD through prayer), come with your hopes high, expecting something from the Most High.
- **Reverence**: You should prepare your heart before you go into His presence. You don't rush into GOD's presence. I wonder why people rush prayers. If you reverence

somebody, you would want to take your time to serve him or her very well. It's the same with GOD. Let the quietness clear away the thoughts of the world. Habakkuk 2:20 says, *"...but the Lord is in His holy temple; let all the earth hush and keep silence before Him."*

- **Alertness**: Be attentive; be ready to hear from the Creator. Be alert; He deserves your full attention. So, give it to Him.
- **Be willing to Obey**: Willingness to obey is a crucial attitude. Come into His presence with a heart to serve and to follow the orders He gives.

There are several ways to grow spiritually. And they involve feeding the physical senses with the right food. Your eyes shouldn't see evil or immorality and your mind should not be happy being exposed to it. Your ears shouldn't accept false teachings and ungodly music. Your tongue shouldn't be comfortable speaking negative of others. You should not give in to lustful desires under the pretense that they are 'emotions.' Here are some additional ways you can grow spiritually:

Reading and studying the Bible. When I was young in faith, the thought of reading the entire bible sounded impossible. Now, there are several good resources which are available to help you do this. If you completed the Bible within a year, you should continue. Do it repeatedly. Team up with others to do so. The best way to feed your mind is by reading. When you read, your mind works. It captures the letters on every page and builds a strong idea in you. Something you cannot really touch or feel but you can see its results. The Bible says that *"The word of GOD is quick (full of life), and powerful..."*[31] You must take the word of GOD very seriously to grow spiritually.

Choose a book of the bible to study: When you read through the bible, you will have a solid foundation and you should build on this foundation. Go beneath the surface; uncover the truths, principles and insights in the scripture. You may want to study one book of the bible each quarter or one for the entire year. You should know the difference between reading and studying. There are several bible apps and study bibles which can help you to study the bible on your own. New Inductive Study Bible, Olive Tree Bible App is one of them.

Study a topic which will help you grow in your relationship with GOD. Ask yourself, where you want to be in your relationship with the Lord by the end of the year? Then you should begin to set tangible goals for getting there. The Bible has been so explored that you just need a single word and you are in another world. For instance, use your bible app to search for a word which keeps coming in your thoughts or spirit. For example, you can search the word, "voice." If you want to learn how to hear GOD's voice, read how others in the biblical times were taught to hear GOD's voice. This is a great process that can help you. Now once you have

---

[31]

initiated your search for the word "voice"; read all the passages that are presented. Then select the one you feel GOD wants you to choose and begin to study that passage in its entirety.

Listen to positive and inspirational messages. Load your phones or iPod with messages from your spiritual leaders. Nowadays, a lot of churches has a media outlet. You can get the podcast of your favorite messages and listen to them repeatedly, instead of loading your phone with negative music which appeals to the carnal emotions. Inspirational messages and spirit-lifting songs should be used to replace them.

Watch messages: Watch messages on YouTube. You can get the messages of popular men of GOD like Bishop Neil C. Ellis, Bishop T.D Jakes, Joel Osteen, etc. Feed your eyes and ears with GOD's word.

Take part in a weekly small group Bible study: This can take place anywhere; at home, in the church and even at work (depending on your kind of job). You may be the one to take the lead among your friends, neighbors, or co-workers. Our spiritual growth moves at a faster rate in a community-based setting because we can share our experiences with one another and hold each other accountable.

Start or join a weekly prayer group: you get the opportunity to join others who share similar concerns with you. For example, if you are a mom, you have a prayer group full of people who pray for their children and spouses. As a single lady, you would find others who are waiting on the Lord for the right partner. Apart from prayer, you receive Godly counsels.

Help yourself by taking time to stop and listen to the advice from others who have achieved what you are trying to achieve in life. Everyone must learn to carry their own baby to full term but along the journey we will encounter others who can coach us to our success. Do you have an ear to hear? I believe we can avoid a high-risk pregnancy when we open ourselves to the right counsel and mentorship. Following the laws and principles of Christ and the advice from those that have spiritual insight, can help you to have a healthier pregnancy.

Keep a journal to record your growth and study notes: Most times we feel this isn't necessary, but I tell you it is. You may have a similar experience in the future and need that right Bible passage to fall back on or a reminder of GOD's victorious power displayed in your life. Your journal would give you that and more. You should include your spiritual discoveries. Be sure to date each page. By the end of the year, you will have a good record of your progress.

Write down your blessings as well as answered prayers: you can include this in the journal or record every blessing in a *"blessings book."* When you do this, you will not only be more keenly aware of how GOD is working in and around your life, but you will also be able to see your progress.

Disciple a young believer: This may look very "big" for someone who is just coming into the knowledge of Christ. We learn the most when we teach others. Seeing people grasp truth for the first time gives a fresh impact on your life too.

GOD's desire for us, is that we grow in the Spirit.

GOD's desire for us, is that we grow in spirit. He desires a strong relationship between man and Himself. Spiritual maturity is being like Christ. Paul The Apostle talks about spiritual maturity in just one phrase. *"...efficient and graceful in response to GOD's Son, fully mature adults, fully developed within and without, fully alive like Christ."*[32] As Christians, we should feel uncomfortable when we are not growing spiritually. In fact, we wouldn't be satisfied with ourselves. Our desire to know more about JESUS, should drive us to grow spiritually. Because to know Him is to love Him, and to love Him causes us to want to spend more time with Him. Our desire to spend more time with Him will push us to *lay aside every weight and sin that could cause us to stumble.*[33]

It is interesting to know that the above-mentioned ways to grow spiritually can work for anybody. Now when we look at ways to grow on a business level you can see similar parallels. If you received a multimillion-dollar business idea, the next thing for you to do is, develop that idea by reading books about your niche. Then dedicate time towards creating a plan of action to manifest it. You also would want to meet others who are successful in business that

---

[32] Ephesians 4:13 (msg)
[33] Hebrews 12:1 (KJV)

can help mentor you and give better insight. Then network with those who believe in your idea and are willing to journey with you through the process to succeed. These are practical ways to grow whether it be spiritually, business, physically or emotionally.

Let me reinforce the power of the scriptures. You can compare and find ways to improve every area of our lives through the bible. I love the bible because it is complete. It has the solution to all challenges of life. We get help from GOD and from the spiritual growth process. Unlike physical growth, which could reach its limit; spiritual growth has no limit on earth. We continue to grow and keep growing. The process of growing spiritually affects our faith.

Exercising My Mind Of Faith

We need help exercising our mind of faith and even before we do so, we also need help building our faith. One thing I know that works in our favor in life and in the business, world is choosing to; BELIEVE. If we don't believe in ourselves, how do we expect others to believe in us? Belief is the seed of faith. If you have faith the size of a mustard seed, you can move mountains![34]

People think being a Christian is going to church and trying not to do any wrong. Well, if that is what you think I invite you to understand the real reason why we are Christian. Being a Christian is being Christ-like. JESUS came to teach us practical ways to live

---

[34] Matthew 17:20

our lives that would honor GOD, ourselves and our neighbors. JESUS died for every sinner. Christ didn't come to establish a religion. He came to establish a lifestyle and the true interpretation of GOD's love towards us.

Most times I tell people that true religion is not a religion at all; it is a way of life (*they usually give me that weird stare*). I know what they mean by that. As Christians, yes, we will continue to practice religion, but until we come to the realization that our faith is not based on religion; we cannot receive salvation.

My father is a pastor. Although I was born into a Godly family, didn't mean I automatically had a full understanding of the faith. I always tagged along with my grandfather; who was a great Deacon. We got up early in the morning, we prayed, we sung. We went to church. The faith was bigger than that. Again, I didn't understand everything about GOD and The Faith, but what I did understand made me want to pursue more! I wanted more! *GOD, Faith, the strong force behind my father's Joy*. I wanted it all!

Why should we understand The Faith? It is so easy to believe in something or someone you don't really understand right? This train of thought is common among religious fanatics. You are a Christian, how has it affected you? You are still yourself what has changed? Your spirit? Your soul?

The truth is that you are a new creation altogether! Your soul changes, your spirit changes and your body as well. You may not believe that last one, but I am telling you the truth. Your body does change. There was a time that GOD used me to minister to a drunkard, he surrendered his life to Christ. We were in a pub. He didn't go to rehab. He didn't attend any social gathering. He surrendered his life and GOD took all of it away. Someone who was a drunk would have an awful look. Christ transformed him into somebody new. I have been meeting him for several years now and the last time I saw him, he was well dressed, well-groomed and he had all the look of a responsible fellow. You cannot separate the spiritual from the practical.

That's just the truth. You must understand your faith. Why did you follow Christ? There are benefits, but I have to say this, the benefits you think GOD can give you, will only come when you know who you are serving. The only way we can know who we are serving is when He reveals himself to us.

Knowing the essentials of The Christian Faith is important here. The essentials to The Christian Faith are the deity of Christ, salvation by GOD's grace and not by works, salvation through JESUS Christ who is the author and finisher of our faith, the resurrection of Christ, the Gospel, monotheism and Holy Trinity.

CHAPTER SIX

SPIRIT VS SOUL

"For the word that GOD speaks is alive and full of power . . . dividing line of the breath of life (soul) and [the immortal] Spirit" Hebrews 12:4

We have established the fact that our spiritual growth is just as important as our physical growth. This affects everything about us. The human body is made up of the spirit and the soul. Both require help from GOD and help from man. Man, here could also mean you and others. Just like all other aspects of our lives, we need help growing our spirit into GOD's standard. *The man without the Holy Spirit does not accept the things that come from the Spirit of GOD; for they are foolishness to him, and he cannot understand them[35].* There is a level that our spirit gets to; where the things of this world are put into its proper perspective . We need help to be able to get to that level.

---

[35] 1 Corinthians 2:14

The spirit and the soul are not the same. They have never been the same since creation. I can recall a Sunday, during Sunday-School. Someone asked a question; "What is the difference between the spirit and the soul?" The question puzzled the members for some 10-15 minutes, until I could say something about it. From the Bible passage above, one could get that Paul was saying that they could be divided by the Word of GOD. If they can be divided, how can you say they are the same? The reason we may not be able to make the appropriate distinction is because we fail to dig deeper into the word of GOD with clarity.

I also remember, some years back, in the western part of the United States, there was a "gold rush." People would rush out west just to get gold most people panned a little gold out of the creeks, some found nuggets lying on the ground and they lazily picked them up. But if you wanted to be very rich, you had to dig for it. This principle applies to spiritual matters. We mentioned that you can read the Bible within a year. You can skim along on the surface of the Bible and you would get little nuggets here and there, but if you really want the Gold, you must dig deep beyond the surface.

I decided to dig deeper into the spiritual realm and on my journey, I ran across good information from Kenneth E. Habin's book *"How You Can Be Led By The Spirit Of GOD."* According to him; with my body I contact the physical realm. With my spirit I contact the spiritual realm. The soul is what contacts the intellectual or soulish realm which includes emotions. We need help connecting to the spiritual realm.

Our understanding and our human mentality are a large portion of our soul. The inward part of man is the candle of the Lord, searching the innermost parts of the belly. JESUS Christ said, *"From his innermost being shall flow [continuously] springs and rivers of living water"*[36] as a result of receiving the Holy Spirit. Praying in another tongue (by the power of the Holy Spirit) is one of the ways to activate your spirit.

As we bring our focus back to exercising our faith. There are two kinds of faith I want to focus on: first is the faith for salvation, I have explained that above. Second is Faith for believe. *'Now faith is the assurance (the confirmation, the title deed) of the things [we] hope for, being the proof of the things [we] do not see and the conviction of their reality [faith perceiving as real fact what is not revealed to the senses].*[37] Exercising your Christian Faith should be a top priority.

Activate Your Faith through times of Adversity

We should always exercise our faith; even in the face of difficulty. As Christians, we encounter many trials. The trials Christians

---

[36] John 7:38 *(NASB)*
[37] Hebrews 11:1

encounter come in different forms and shapes and they would need different levels of faith. There are different trials which affect different parts of our spiritual life. We call them challenges. They could affect the believer and even the church. They could be responsible for several things. In fact, what motivated me to write this book was a spiritual challenge I went through early on in ministry. I knew about being pregnant spiritually and giving birth to destiny. I ran into a lot of challenges trying to birth my blessing. So, I started investigating about the birthing process and how a person conceived a child. I was also curious to know what causes a miscarriage and what are the risk signs before one happens. I found out that a miscarriage takes place before the full development of an organism matures enough to survive outside the womb. When I thought about this on a spiritual level, I knew for sure, that I was pregnant with destiny. I knew I was pregnant with purpose, yet, it seemed like the challenges that I was going through was about to kill everything before my "baby" could develop and mature. I have learned over time, that how we respond to trials, determines our level of faith. It also gives us the ability to exercise our faith. Trials pierce through the soul; they minister "grief" and they are very painful. Being guarded by GOD doesn't always mean that these trials won't come. In fact, GOD allows it, but for our good.

But put forth Your hand now, and touch his bone and his flesh, and he will curse and renounce you to Your face. And the Lord said to Satan, Behold, he is in your hand; only spare his life.[38]

Can you get the picture here? GOD was proud of His son (Job). And the devil was trying to tell Him (GOD) that Job is only serving Him because of what He has given him. Hence the statement *"Put forth your hand, touch his bone and his flesh . . ."* and what did GOD say? "Behold, he is in your (the devil) hand; only spare his life".

Now, one may ask, If GOD is so good, why do we pass through pains? First, GOD didn't say pains wouldn't come. Paul understood this and that was why he said, *"The Lord will deliver me out of every evil work, and will save me for his heavenly kingdom, to whom be the glory forever and ever. Amen"*[39] Peter assured us; *"Beloved, do not be surprised by the fiery trials among you (that have come for the purpose of testing you), as though a strange thing has happened to you"*[40]. The next verse tells us to rejoice! *"But insofar as you are sharing Christ's sufferings, rejoice, so that when His glory [full of radiance and splendor] is revealed, you may also rejoice with triumph [exultantly]."* Our faith is compared to gold; it must be exposed to fire before it comes out refined and beautiful like the gold, we all know. The day I saw a nugget of gold, I couldn't

---

[38] *JOB 2:6 (Amplified Bible)*

[39] 2 Tim 4:18
[40] 1 Peter 4:12

believe my eyes. It was so "un-gold" Our faith in its raw form is so "un-faith". It must pass through fire to become the FAITH.

When you focus on Christ rather than the trial, you will experience a taste of heaven on earth amidst your trial. We should exercise our Christian faith, even in the face of difficulty; in challenges and even at the loss of someone very close. In fact, that is when we really need to exercise our faith. The writer to the Hebrews exhorts the Christians of his day who encountered much trials and he is still exhorting us even today. *"We do not want you to become sluggish, but to imitate those who through faith and patience inherit what has been promised"*[41] Again he writes, *"Let us hold fast the confession of our hope without wavering, for he who promised is faithful"*[42]

Having a calling is a duty, a responsibility and not a title. When we receive the calling, we must faith walk into action immediately; Or it would be like having a dream and not taking the right steps to make it a possibility. Mark Twain, one of my favorite fictional authors said, *"Twenty years from now you will be more disappointed by the things that you didn't do than the ones you did do. So, throw off the bowlines. Sail away from the safe harbor. Catch the trade winds in your sails. Explore! Dream! Discover!"*

How can you strengthen your faith? I am a strong believer in having the right, positive people around me. When GOD places the right people in your life to give you that word of encouragement or

---

[41]Hebrews 6:12
[42] Hebrews 10:23.

that advice, they can help you get over the hump in your life. They can strengthen your faith.

Secondly, be ready to share your experiences with others. Keep them close and tell them what is going on. You should take this part carefully and cautiously, telling the wrong people could bring more pain. GOD is going to help you by using the right people around you.

Visualizing the appearance of my Baby

Vision is a secret shared by most successful people in life, the athletes, CEOs, actors and mothers too. Arnold Schwarzenegger had this to say; *"All I know is that the first step is to create a vision, because when you see the vision-the beautiful vision-that creates the want power."*

Paul the apostle prayed that the eyes of our understanding may be opened[43], What happens when your eyes are opened? You begin to see of course. You need help when it comes to seeing vision. GOD may lay it in your heart to do something and to take your family along too. What happens when you just have the idea and you don't know the driving force behind it? Your vision becomes vague. We need help to keep our dreams alive. Visualization helps to keep your vision alive. Oprah, one of the most

---

[43] Ephesians 1:18

successful women of our time, believes in the power of the mind, through visualization; to achieve one's heart's desires.

What are visualizations? Which means to envision The or form a mental picture of something. Basically, seeing something in our mind's eye. Visualization is the product of imagination and we use it naturally when we; sleep (in our dreams), wander from a boring meeting, think of what we want for dinner, try to remember where we parked etc. In fact, visualization works for everything and almost anything.

Your imagination could help you in the following ways;

- It helps you to remember things,
- Makes you anticipate happy things in future
- Gives you the ability to be pessimistic and worry
- It could inspire solutions to problems
- Makes your idea spicy and gives something new to something old
- Allows you to tell others what has happened to you successfully. (It helps you to give good account of the past.)
- It makes you see the beauty in physical things or abstract ideas.

Everyone has an imagination and because of this, everyone can visualize things. Do you doubt that? Take a deep relaxing breath now. Close your eyes or you can leave them open. Think of where you kept your keys. Think of the person you love most. Think about what is in your refrigerator presently. Good, encourage yourself with a clap because you just made use of your imagination. Don't let us get our facts wrong here. Imagination is quite different from visualization, even though only a thin line of difference exists between them. Images formed in the head may look like a snap shot or could even be like a full-color motion picture. Most of the time, we rarely take cognizance of these mental pictures they happen so often and come by so quickly.

In the medical world, visualizing and imagining the delivery date or even the sex of your baby is not really needed because of technological advances like the sonogram. However, even with that, when you spend time visualizing your childbirth, you are preparing your mind and body to handle the experience. Why do we need to visualize the appearance of the baby or the appearance of the ministry? It is said that expectation is the mother of manifestation. If we can think of it, then it can happen. When my wife was pregnant, I remember one day when we sat down together thinking about how our child would grow up, places we would take them and how rooted in the word they would be. One of the greatest things GOD deposited in man was the mind. When we put our imaginations into spiritual work, it becomes Godly Imagination. Visualizations becomes the eyes of our hearts and this is where GOD can help us see a snapshot of our blessing before it manifests in the earth realm.

We need help if we want to have Godly imaginations which could affect our visualizations. One process affects the other and the decline in one could mean the decline in the other. Sometimes, I hear young believers battle with what we know as 'negative or bad thoughts.' Well, there is something I must say about this, when you have the right positive seeds, you can bear Godly fruit. *"Out of the abundance of the heart, the mouth speaketh[44]."* Fill your heart with the right things and these 'negative or bad thoughts' will leave. If you help yourself and accept GOD's for help, you will achieve your goal.

Looking through the Bible, GOD gave Abraham a vision of the stars of the sky and He told him he would have that many offspring and this visual aid produced faith in GOD's plan for in his heart[45]. What a perfect example of Godly imagery perfected in the visualizations of the eyes of our heart. The Most High has created us with eyes in our hearts and with which we can see, picture and visualize what He has planned for us. He desires for us to fill these eyes with His dreams, visions, and destiny.

Seeing visions and dreams is one of the works of the eyes of the heart. Our Lord JESUS Christ filled our eyes with visualizations. He filled the ears of His listeners by constantly teaching in parables[46]. In fact, our world as a Christian is full of visualizations. When we pray, meditate, sing hymns, we have an angelic picture in our hearts, that is the work of visualization. A picture is worth a thousand words. This means that seeing is far better than telling. When you see something, it has a more powerful effect than just hearing about it. In the Book of Acts GOD Himself worked on the physical eyes

---

[44] MATTHEW 12:34
[45] Genesis 15:5
[46] Matthew 13:34

of Paul the Apostle. After that encounter, Paul (Saul) was never the same. GOD touched the eyes of his heart.

Visualization also works in dreams. GOD counsels us at night through our dreams[47]. During our time of rest, GOD will speak life and reveal secrets that we can see.

See Your Vision Succeeding: Ideas Coming Into Fruition

Visualizing the appearance of your "baby" will create a necessary sense of expectation. Expectation will cause you to enter a state of preparation. Expectation through faith places a demand on GOD to perform that which He spoke into your spirit; preparation tells GOD you are ready to receive it. All of this is sparked by the fire of visualization. Constantly seeing your vision from the finish line will push you to that finish line.

The Holy Spirit will open your eyes to the will of GOD for your life and cause you to see into the super natural. The bible says that, "He [Christ] would send a helper, intercessor, advocate, strengthener and standby, that He may remain with you forever..." The Holy Spirit is our help in the visualization of our dreams, gift, ideas and our "baby" (the ministry/business/ purpose). Submitting to the Holy Spirit daily will help us enormously. He not only will help us to see what GOD has planned, but will lead, guide and direct us into the place of manifestation. When we get discouraged and feel like giving up, He sends us a visual reminder of what the finish line

---

[47] Psalms 16:7

looks like. Remember, seeing yourself on the other side of the finish line will get you to that line! So, see yourself successful! See the momentum of your ministry! See your business booming! See your dreams coming into a now reality! Seeing it will give you the strength to run, climb, build, fight and make it to the place of purpose.

CHAPTER SEVEN

Symptoms of a Miscarriage

Our body naturally gives signs when an abnormality creeps in. Symptoms are warning signs and once we experience one, we should cry for help immediately. This should be the response that happens to all aspects of our lives. Sometimes we may feel that we are on the verge of losing the bond in our marriage. We can even go through that feeling that our business is going to have to be liquidated. Attack it before it gets out of hand. When you feel something strange, you should cry for help right away.

Before a miscarriage happens, we have symptoms. Miscarriage is a term used for a pregnancy that ends on its own, within the first 20 weeks of gestation. In a bid to use the right euphemism we may refer to it as *pregnancy loss*. According to the American College of Obstetricians and Gynecologist (ACOG), 10-25% of all clinically recognized pregnancies end in miscarriage. Chemical pregnancies are what happen when pregnancy is lost shortly after implantation within 50-70% of all miscarriages. Statistically, most miscarriages occur during the first 13 weeks of pregnancy. During the first trimester which is from the 1st week to the 14th week of pregnancy, the most common cause of miscarriage is chromosomal abnormality which means that there is a malfunction present in the chromosomes responsible for pregnancy. Chromosomal abnormalities cause the egg to be damaged or even the sperm cell and this could happen at the time the zygote went through the division process. Other causes of miscarriage could include; hormonal problems, infections or maternal health problems, lifestyle-smoking, drug use, malnutrition, excessive caffeine and exposure to radiation or toxic substance, implantation of the egg into the uterine lining fails to occur properly, maternal trauma.

Is miscarriage the fault of the woman or the child? According to Professor Lesley Regan, author of Miscarriage-What Every Woman Needs To Know, 'The common reasons for miscarriage are genetic abnormalities in the embryo or an infection in the mother. *Pregnancy loss is the body's way of ending a pregnancy that cannot continue normally. Although it is a common occurrence, this does not take away from the deep sense of loss and hurt it causes, we should be offering empathy and support to couples suffering from such loss, not accusing them of bringing it on."* During spiritual miscarriage, there is no time to apportion blame to the devil or the believer. Remember that we said a miscarriage is a physical loss which affects our spiritual life and demise of the products of the Holy Spirit leading to unbelief and weak faith as well as backsliding.

Entrepreneurs, artists and even writers do have ideamiscarriage. They could be likened to *project death*. You may have a multimillion-dollar idea and the execution of it becomes a flop because of the lack of consistency in properly nurturing the idea. Have you ever wondered why companies liquidate? Have you ever wondered why ideas fail? The answer is quite simple! They all failed to take note of miscarriage warning signs. This chapter would teach you how to recognize pregnancy loss warning signs.

Some major signs of having a natural pregnancy loss include:

- When back pain becomes severe from mild and could be worse than normal menstrual cramps
- Weight loss could be a factor here
- White-pink mucus
- Frequently occurring contractions especially when they happen every 5-20 minutes
- Bright red bleeding with or without cramps as well as Brown bleeding. Even though 20-30% of all pregnancies can experience some bleeding in the early stage but 50% of these could result to normal pregnancies
- Clot like tissues or materials begin to pass from the vagina
- When a decrease in signs of pregnancy occurs

The health care professional advises you to call your doctor or even the hospital right away if you are experiencing the above symptoms. I totally agree but with this one addition; contact the Bible. This may sound irrational to you, especially for someone who finds it hard to believe the bible. Try it, Search the scriptures.

> "The midwives answered Pharaoh, Because the Hebrew women are not like the Egyptian women; they are vigorous and quickly delivered; their babies are born before the midwife comes to them"
>
> EXODUS 1:19 (*Amplified Bible*)

The Hebrew women gave birth safely and no incidence of miscarriage was recorded while they were in Egypt and even after they left. What is this telling us? GOD is available to strengthen us, to give us the help we need during the trimesters of pregnancy. Even in the face of immediate threat to the baby, from an attacker.

There are several types of pregnancy loss. And these would be explained according to spiritual and physical loss:

1. **Threatened Miscarriage:** This happens when some degree of early pregnancy uterine bleeding accompanied by cramping or lower backache occurs. The bleeding is often because of implantation and the cervix remains closed. Threatened miscarriage could be treated with Acetaminophen (Tylenol) and it may also lead to surgery. Threatened loss of pregnancy should be handled before it gets out of hand.

   As humans we have instincts, our gut feelings. Sometimes it could be the work of the Holy Spirit. You may just feel so uncomfortable taking a step in the execution of your ideas. You should be sensitive to your feelings and the spirit of Christ. The Holy Spirit will lead you and guide you into all truth. John 16:13 ... *and He will announce and declare to you the things that are to come [that will happen in the future]* Threatened pregnancy loss could be controlled. Identifying the threat will give you a target for prayer. And remember No weapon formed against you shall prosper!!! That includes every threat, just like the Hebrew women's unborn babies was threatened by Pharaoh- GOD intervened. GOD will also intervene for you!

At the second trimester stage, miscarriages could be caused by unmanaged diabetes, high blood pressure, lupus, kidney diseases, thyroid problems, infections, Rubella, Cytomegalovirus (CMV), STD, Malaria, food poisoning, Fibroids, weakened cervix, Polycystic ovary Syndrome (PCOS) etc. We should also know that threatened miscarriage could be prevented by; avoiding alcohol, not smoking, managing high blood pressure, managing diabetes, getting infections treated etc. Threatened pregnancy loss happen to our purpose, ideas and businesses. When we are pregnant with GOD's purpose, the devil may try to send a threatened miscarriage. This is when we need to have the senses.

The Holy Spirit paired with our natural senses gives us what I call INSTINCT. The way T.D Jakes puts it in his book- Instincts; "you just know". When something is about to happen, you just know. We are all born with instincts, a person is more likely to be born without sight than to not possess insight. Our blind friends make use of this insight. Present in us, is our internal senses which are beyond the physical, even though they work majorly on the physical. These senses determine what is right, what is safe and what's next. It is important for us to pay attention to these senses as they speak to us all day. They help us to sidestep danger and to seize opportunities. The Holy Spirit heightens these senses. He makes them work in an extraordinary way. GOD laterally begins to talk to you, and you hear Him speak through your physical ears (not just in your hearts or mind this time around). It is a glorious experience that I have longed for when I was a young Christian and I was so happy when it did!

GOD created the heavens and the earth, there is nothing beyond His reach. Any threat should be nullified with prayer and The Word of GOD. Besides, such threat should be avoided even before it comes your way, because of the Spirit of Christ in you.

2. **Inevitable or incomplete Miscarriage:** This kind of pregnancy loss is marked with abdominal or back pain and is usually accompanied by bleeding with an open cervix. Pregnancy loss becomes inevitable when there is a dilation or effacement of the cervix or when the rupture of the membranes happens. The bleeding and cramps could continue if the miscarriage is not complete.

Can someone really be pregnant with GOD's purpose and lose the baby? I guess you know the answer to that, but the question should be this- can GOD be so "cruel" to cause a miscarriage? I wouldn't want to give an answer for that, but I leave that to the spirit of Christ in you or better still - Your INSTINCTS. When something becomes inevitable it becomes very hard to avoid or totally impossible. If it is completely impossible to avoid it, why should we even try? Because we can't just let it happen, even if it appears to be impossible to deflect. Besides, GOD has not destined any evil to anyone. His thoughts and plans are of good and not of evil[48]. It all comes down to making the right decision, the decision to line up with the will and plans of GOD. He says, "See, I set before you today life and prosperity, death and destruction . . ."[49] Therefore, success depends on your choice. You didn't become pregnant with purpose, just to lose it. You are here for a reason. I hear some people say things like; *the idea is bound to fail*. No idea is bound to fail; in fact, we don't fail, we only learn new ways of doing things better. Robert H. Schuller said, *"If there exist no possibility of failure, then victory is meaningless."* This powerful truth applies to all aspects of our life, both spiritual and physical. So, when you are faced with any incomplete or inevitable pregnancy loss, you should understand that there

---

[48] Jeremiah 29:11
[49] Deuteronomy 30:19

is not failure in GOD! And if He placed that "baby" in you, it must come forth!

3. **Missed-miscarriage:** Women can experience this kind of pregnancy loss even without knowing it. What happens is that the embryonic death happens but there is not any expulsion of the embryo. No one knows why this occurs. A loss of pregnancy symptoms would be the sign of the absence of fetal heart tones when tested through an ultrasound. Could this happen when we are pregnant with a purpose? Could we possibly lose our purpose without knowing it? When our vision, ministry, ideas or business dies slowly, a possible missed-miscarriage must have happened. How does it take place?

- When we are comfortable with not fulfilling it.
- The fire in us dies.
- We become satisfied with the current state of things.
- We leave the comfort Christ has provided and we bury ourselves in our own comfort, our own belief and fulfillment.

When these things happen, we find it hard to move forward. We are neither getting better nor deteriorating, we are stagnant. *So, because you are lukewarm-neither hot nor cold - I am about to spit you out of my mouth*[50].

When you feel that your dreams and visions are drifting away, consult GOD! Cry to him for help! In response, he will answer and rekindle your spirit with a burning fire. Tap into that burning fire, it will propel you to operating beyond your imagination.

Unexpected pains: Misunderstandings

During pregnancy, some pains may become inevitable as they are completely natural, while others could be resulting from something else. Abdominal pain is one symptom that women often complain about during pregnancy. However, it is normal to complain about it because it is an indication of a deep-rooted pathology which is taking place inside a woman's body. It is normal to experience abdominal pain with mood swings, backache and food craving, because the baby and organs are launched in the lower part of the abdomen. Why does a woman experience upper abdominal pain? Simple, the position where the uterus is situated is the area around which the pain would be felt, besides you have a new life in you, he/she is trying to build some organs. The woman is trying to balance her life and that of the baby. Any pain during pregnancy

---

[50] Rev 3:16 *NIV*

should be addressed. The expecting mother is strongly advised to visit the doctor once she experiences any pain.

Likewise, in carrying purpose, sometimes "pains" come unexpectedly. They just come without any announcement and you must deal with them. My Grandfather's death was one of such unexpected pain. He was more than a grandfather to me. He was my spiritual compass and what happens when you lose your compass in the middle of the sea? You look to the stars, sun and the heavenly bodies for help. I did lose my compass on earth and this made me must look to GOD for help.

Unexpected pains can come from anywhere; from partners, family, friends, even your role models or mentors just to name a few. 'Pains could come from anyone who is offering his/her "sincere" opinions about your "baby". Some already foresee. a miscarriage even before implantation. How could this be rectified? Unfortunately, it cannot. You can only control it. Lack of conviction and courage is what propels "pregnancy loss". Just because they that *the idea is dumb and wouldn't work* doesn't mean it wouldn't. You must remover that *"GOD will work the will and do of his good pleasure"*.[51] In other words, you are not alone. GOD is your help! I'm not telling you to ignore sound wisdom; but I implore you to know that difference between wisdom and straight out negativity. Wisdom builds, negativity pulls down.

---

[51] Philippians 2:13 KJV

Abraham Lincoln said, *"Determine that the thing can and shall be done, and then we shall find the way."* Sometimes instead of our friends and family members giving us active support, they (hopefully- unknowingly) offer "pains". A few These "pains" may come through:

1) Debilitating criticism
2) Discouragement
3) No vote of confidence

From another point of view, don't allow the discouragement of no support cause unnecessary "pains" to your "baby". To be honest, you should not expect support from everyone all the time. Reason one being, it is quite possible that these people have other things and problems going on in their life. I wouldn't hold it against them. Reason two, they may not have the capacity to give you the support you need. People can't give what they don't have.

What's important is, identifying your support needs. Moral support, physical support, emotional support, intellectual support and resource support. You may need all or some of these mentioned. Take a piece of paper, write down the category of support and the specific details you need.

Now, begin to connect the dots with whom each support is best to come from. For example, when it comes to moral and spiritual support, the Holy Spirit is the best one to provide it. Physical support could be very difficult because that requires community, someone to spend time with you. The point is, support is needed. It's important to network and meet new people and even reacquaint yourself with those whom you already know. Then match your support needs to their gifting and specialties. Don't be afraid to ask for help! Communicate clearly what your needs are. Be sure to find out what they need in return from you in order to solidify their commitment to your vision.

Again, it is best to connect and surround yourself with like-minded people. You'll meet with people who are working on the same goal or similar ones. After taking the time to prove their character; share your ideas and share your goals. See how they may connect with theirs. Caution, at this point you need to be careful, you don't want to give your "baby" to a thief. Remembering what we dealt with previously, you also don't want to open yourself to a bunch of negativity or evil counsel proposed to derail your vision. Therefore, we should not remove GOD's part here as He could turn the counsel of the ungodly into foolishness. *"Now David had been told, "Ahitophel is among the conspirators with Absalom." So, David prayed, "O LORD turn Ahithophel's counsel into foolishness."*[52]

Though we indeed need support, understand that some people just won't "get it", period! They won't see your vision, not because you didn't communicate effectively, but because they already decided they would not. Don't get discourage by this, instead celebrate it. Wear it as a badge of honor and join the exclusive club of pioneers.

---

[52] II Samuel 15 (NIV)

"History show us that the people who end up changing the world- the great political, social, scientific, technological, artistic, even sports revolutionaries-are always nuts, until they are right, and then they are geniuses" -John Eliot

Whenever you are getting opposition from people about your vision and forces are trying to stop you from reaching progress; it could mean that, there is great value hidden in your goal. When you finally achieve your goal, some really great things are in store for you. When I received the call into the ministry, my friends and family rejoiced with me and they were happy for me. The gospel of salvation was the foundation of our family.

Sometimes, when we pursue things that really matter to us, or things that look brand new to us, a path we have never been, we begin to feel more *sensitive* and *vulnerable* than usual; we are walking in an unknown territory so naturally, we are apprehensive. This causes us to seek validation and support from others, more than we really need to. There are friends and family not being supportive, because they are simply behaving the way they are. People's discouragement reflects their inner fears and beliefs. One weakness that I have struggled with my entire life is a speech impediment. This disability has been a constant thorn in my flesh over the years. I can remember kids in school made fun of me. It really made me feel bad. It has affected my confidence, my ability to engage with certain people and organizations. I'm sure some thought I was being "shady" or stuck-up, and it has caused me to miss out on opportunities because in many cases I felt that I wasn't qualified enough to speak at certain events; due of my speech impediment.

When I was in middle school, I had a teacher, who assisted me in my speech; her name was Sherry Magee. She is still supportive of me. When she sees me, she encourages me to let me know how much I have improved over the years, and that she is proud of me. She was there to make me a better person. She does so even to this day.

Have you read the story of Moses and Aaron? It is a beautiful story that showcased how Aaron helped Moses' with his speech impediment. See GOD has a way of providing the help we need in the areas we may be weak in. This is why we should trust Him. Trust the spirit of Christ in us and follow His footsteps. After all, we didn't get pregnant on our own. We are pregnant with His purpose. He is going to help to become great parent and our baby will grow up in the LORD.

CHAPTER EIGHT

Panic Attack

Help! I am having a panic attack. Why do panic attacks come? How can we prevent panic attacks? Who do we call when we have panic attacks?

Panic attacks, during pregnancy are devastating. Panic attacks are essentially periods of serious or intense mental stress, which can be combined with very real physical symptoms. To such extent that many are hospitalized over concerns that they are suffering from a heart attack. A panic attack seems worse when pregnant because you are already suffering from an emotional and stressful state. You are concerned about your baby and even yourself. Stressful pregnancy and worries about the future are products of panic attack. Panic attacks are not as dangerous on their own, but when they come during pregnancy, they become two different problems embedded in one. They can lead to physical and mental stress; which would in turn affect the fetus' development in the womb. There are several causes of pregnancy panic attacks.

Some of which are; hormonal fluctuations, health anxiety, previous panic attacks etc.

This element of miscarriage or pregnancy loss itself is a bit of a mystery to scientific research. Researchers have been able to discover the issues which causes panic attacks, but there is no clear reason for happening more frequent for some than others. They are just more prone to panic attacks than others. Scientists know the reasons why pregnant women get panic attacks, but the part which fails to be clear is, why some pregnant women are just more prone to panic attacks than others. Most likely, there could exist some genetic ability to have a panic attack; which affects some. Other people just have their own level of anxiety. We can't deny that bringing a life into this world is very stressful. Most women who become pregnant may experience happiness at first but may have worries once they think of the amount of work and the responsibility which follows and or the uncontrollable variables of life.

As a pastor, a business person, a spouse, and a parent. You could fall under the effects of a panic attack and if you fail to seek help, the results may be devastating. In the book of Luke twelfth chapter; JESUS encouraged us not to worry about what was out of our control, but instead to trust in GOD. For the most part, it's stressing-out over the "unknown" and the uncontrollable, that for the most part, leads to a panic attack.

I came across this bible passage (Luke 12:22-26) when I was early in faith and I have never let it go. Whenever I read it, it turns all my anxiety into a meaningless rumble. Again, panic attacks usually begin with the "what if" notion. The "what if" questions are one of the hardest parts of pregnancy. There is little or nothing we can do to stop these questions. We must recognize that these questions exist, and we should not give in to them. Doing the following could stop panic attacks: Regular checkups, learning more about panic attacks, relaxation, exercises, and having fun.

Surprisingly, the solutions to panic attack are just too simple to make them feel so important. With such a simple solution, we must not allow fear or anxiety to overwhelm us. Fear leads to anxiety, anxiety leads to panic attack. When we allow panic attack to wreak havoc on us:

- o we begin to question our abilities to parent our baby;
- o we start to second guess our abilities to do the job of parenting;
- o We allow for the spirit of doubt to dwell in us.

All the above will affect how we see our pregnancy. It may even lead to a miscarriage. I made mention of Moses previously, he had his own portion of anxiety. This made him shy away from the "pregnancy". GOD was ready to use him and that was why He continued to show him signs, to affirm him and ensure Moses that he wasn't alone in this "pregnancy".

Panic attacks may come during pregnancy or even after pregnancy. Similarly, it could come in the preliminary stage of being pregnant with GOD's purpose or when we want to deliver-execute that purpose. We could possibly be second guessing our abilities to parent GOD's baby. But remember we are pregnant with GOD's purpose, it is not our will but GOD's will. He would not give us a job He knows we can't complete. When it comes to the business world and we might be having doubts about the idea GOD has laid in our hearts. Whatsoever, form it comes in, get through with it. Sometimes too much thinking could make things go wrong. Trust GOD to do the thinking and you do the following.

"Just because you feel lost doesn't mean that you are. Sometimes you just must relax, breathe deep, and trust the path you're on." -
Lalah

Panic attacks could be brought on by these questions and concerns:

- *What if it becomes a failure?*
- *What if GOD is not with me?*
- *What if I don't reach where He wants me to reach?*
- *What if I stop halfway and I am not able to deliver this baby?*
- *What if I have a miscarriage?*
- *What if! What if! What if!*

You should replace these "what if's" with the statement; *With GOD, all things are possible*[53].

- ✓ With GOD, I wouldn't become a failure!
- ✓ With GOD I would reach my Goal!
- ✓ With GOD I would be able to deliver this baby!

---

[53] Matthew 19:26

- ✓ With GOD I wouldn't have a miscarriage!
- ✓ With GOD! With GOD! With GOD all things would happen according to His plan and purpose!

Worrying: Am I really prepared for Parenting?

Statistics have it that more than 4 million babies are born in this country each year and majority of them arrive healthy and full-term. But this doesn't stop the pregnant women from worrying about everything! Worrying and anxiety dominates the pregnancy world. In fact, there are several types of worries and the most common would be listed below. Even though this part is focused on worrying about parenting, we would have to take the liberty to discuss some of them. Your stress could affect the baby and the worries could affect the child. However, Dr. O'Brien has this to say; *"However, the everyday stress of not being able to pay off a credit-card bill or juggling work and family issues won't cause birth defects or preterm labor"* Another worry could be accidentally harming the fetus before knowing that you are pregnant. Could that be possible?

The fact is that no doctor would ever recommend that a woman should take alcohol or drink during pregnancy but what happens is that moms-to-be do these frequently. If you had one or two drinks weeks before you knew you are pregnant, it doesn't affect the baby. Stay with me, I am going somewhere with all these worries. *"Although there is no amount of alcohol that is considered safe for a growing fetus, if you had one or two drinks in the weeks before you knew you'd conceived, it shouldn't affect your baby's organ development,"* says Dr. O'Brien.

The worry that you would lose it in labor. Pamela Berens, M.D., professor of obstetrics and gynecology at The University of Texas Health Science Center at Houston said that "Childbirth classes aren't just about teaching breathing technique, they are also about showing you what is available for pain relief and how the hospital works as well as what would happen if you need a C-section. Labor hurts, but that doesn't mean that women who go into labor don't survive the pain. They do, they come out strong and the voice of the child and the mother is heard. From the first worry case to the end, none adds any complexity to the birthing process. Simply put, worrying adds nothing to the issue on ground and it removes nothing.

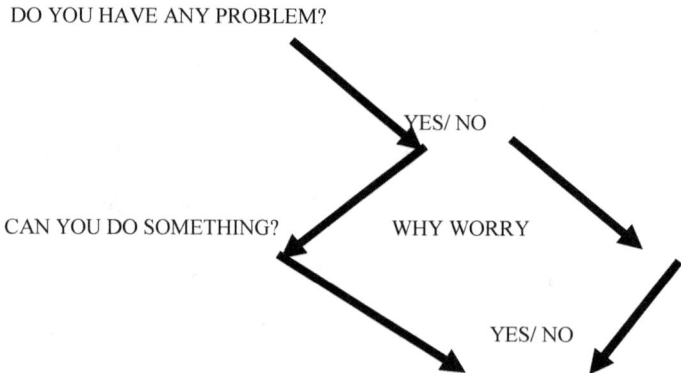

Worrying forms a cycle. Nothing more, nothing less. Our list would be incomplete without mentioning the fear of miscarriage. It is the strongest cause, women worry about.

Kimberly – "I cannot even list all the fear I have with this pregnancy-my first. I will spend the entire day WORRYING that every strange cramp, every fleeting backache is leading me straight to miscarriage.

We all know that parenting isn't a day's job. Like every parent we look at our pockets. Can we afford this baby? An anonymous source discloses that; *like many parents, I am fearful of the money situation. Both my husband and I work; however, I make more money and have better insurance. I used to be an educator and have a firm belief that children do better with a parent at home.* The fear of not being a good parent continues to haunt each woman. Here is what Cate has to say;

"I've been given the precious task of cultivating this incredible new life within me. And like so many parents before me, I am challenged to offer my child the best of this world. I yearn for her to be always bright and happy. And I just find myself wondering where to begin. Most times, I fret over articles written for and in her best interest and worry over the reported statistics of this and that. What is best? In this world where children bore easily, have too much just too soon, and even resort to violence when they realize that life is unfair and difficult, I seek answers and guidance for doing it right."

Being prepared for parenting means, getting our physical and mental state ready for the Baby. The same works for business ideas, goals, visions, aspirations and targets. We need to prepare our mental and physically to be ready for the baby. When we become pregnant with GOD's purpose our anxiety increases and we begin to ask, "Am I really prepared for parenting?" Are you really prepared to handle GOD's project? Yes, you are! GOD has a readily given us all that we need. When it comes to the ministry of Christ, GOD has given us all what we need to parent it. Remember JESUS said that- "He has overcome the world. . .[54]" In other words JESUS was telling us that; *whatever it is, that you will pass through in this world, I have overcome it, and because I have, you can and will also.* The Holy Spirit is there to help us too. He would direct us and be our guide to all truth. He was present during creation. He understands the world and He has a direct connection to our Heavenly Father. GOD the Father is both the biological and physical father of the world. And we have Him as our father, what more do we need in parenting?

---

[54] St John 16:33

CHAPTER NINE

Help So I Can Deliver My Baby

After preparation, presentation follows. This stage like every other stage requires help from people and GOD. We may attempt to hide from the final execution stage, but it will always eventually come and find us. I remember excelling to the twelfth grade in high school. In that last year I began to experience "senioritis?" I worked hard through all those years of grade school and during the last few weeks of school, I didn't feel like studying for my senior finals. Although I was ready for my graduation, there was still that last push of action, I had to complete in order to reach my goal. I am so glad that I had supportive parents and teachers that helped me push to the end.

Like most pregnant women, you are going to reach a certain point during pregnancy when you've had enough, especially during the third trimester. You have enough of being pregnant. You would have had enough of waiting to meet the little person you've been growing for a good solid nine months.

The last trimester of pregnancy remains the most complex of all. Even though it is such an exciting time and a relieving one for that matter, we all bear it in mind that anything could happen during labor. A full-term pregnancy is between 37 to 42 weeks and only 3-5% of babies are born on their estimated due date. A whopping sum of 40% of babies are born before their estimated due date and another 40% after their estimated due dates.

When the delivery day comes, help can come from unexpected places. There is nothing like having a perfect delivery. Even though we get excited when it is time for delivery, our excitement is laced with worries and skepticism. Have you ever been in the waiting room with a dad waiting for the baby to be born, how about a friend and or partner? They would keep pacing the floor? The anxiety is especially here when he is told that there is a complication and he might have to leave the delivery room. Men who watch their wives deliver provide the support she needs. They find out that they can't do anything other than to hold her hand and encourage her to do the needful- PUSH! Help from his side is limited to encouraging words and maybe prayers. In Exodus 1:19, The Hebrew women are easily delivered of their baby because they receive help. Not from the midwives but from GOD himself. I love the KJV of that verse; *and the midwives said unto Pharaoh, because the Hebrew women are not as the Egyptian women; for they are LIVELY, and are delivered before the midwives come in unto them.* Did I just mention *lively*? Yes, I did. Now, let's take that literally.

Have you ever seen a woman in the labor room smiling to the husband while she forces the child out? How possible is it to be lively when it comes to delivery? How possible is it to smile when you are in the rigorous and vigorous work of PUSHING? Who's help do you really need so that you can deliver your baby? GOD's help or that of your spouse? Labor is work, real work and we can't do it on our own, except if we are Hebrew women of course. However, even the Hebrew women got their help from GOD.

Being pregnant with GOD's purpose isn't easy. The dream and vision didn't die in us. We have been able to carry it for more than "nine months". And with His help we will be able to see it till the end.

Now, in the entrepreneurial world, your baby could be a strategy and the execution of that strategy becomes a problem. Statistically, 80% of strategies employed, lack good execution. This is because many entrepreneurs allow themselves to become swept up in putting out fires, instead of executing their daily goals. Setting your priorities right, collecting and analyzing data, keeping a rhythm to meetings and evaluating the strategy are good ways of strategy execution. Your baby needs help, just like you. There are several ways you can help yourself: finding a soothing environment, choosing your team carefully (good doctors, nurses, partners, etc.), learning about labor, expressing your fears by speaking to those involved (don't be deceived, speaking with a knowledgeable and trusted friend practically brings relief and calms your fears), practicing rhythmic breathing, making use of imagery as well as visualization, taking a warm shower or bath, keep moving and seeking relief with warm or cool compresses. All these require help. You can only receive help when you ask for it. You need help all the way; from the first stage to the last; from the fertilization process to parenting, you need GOD's help.

HELP! I Can't Do This By Myself!

We made mention of seeking help when it comes to labor or delivery. For the sake of clarity and to avoid duplication of ideas, this part would focus on the personal needs to push forth your baby. Strength, love and reassurance are needed when it comes to child delivery. This is also needed to execute GOD's purpose for our lives. Being pregnant, carrying the baby for months and delivery seem to be the end of it all. However, there exists a fourth trimester. Before we arrive at that trimester, we would have passed through the birthing stage. As a mother and a father, we would need to check out the Godly characteristics we need to imbibe to make us ready for birthing.

During labor, several things could go wrong, and they vary from woman to woman, from one phase to another, from one labor to another. You are unique in your pregnancy and in your labor; your expectations and feelings will and should be different from others. The people who support and attend to you and the place in which you labor will also affect you.

When in labor, your labor contractions and body movements, as well as your pushing efforts, will guide the baby down as the child flexes, stretches and rotates to explore the birth canal. From the softening (ripening) and opening (dilation) of your cervix, the birth process progresses. When you are close to delivery during the pre-labor stage, your body gets ready for birth.

Strength, love and reassurance will find its way to the labor room when you have the right people with you. The same thing applies to being pregnant with GOD's purpose and making the necessary delivery. The right people will surely come to you if you've taken time to prepare your team. *"Coming together is a beginning. Keeping together is a progress. Working together is a success."* That is one of my favorite quotes from Henry Ford. It explains the importance of team work in a very simple manner.

When labor comes, it is time to gather your support people. It becomes a time to call your provider if you are having a home birth, or to prepare to go to the birth center/hospital. A careful phone consultation or a home visit from any member of your team would go a long way. When you are admitted into the hospital during the early labor stage, it becomes very good for you as studies show that being admitted to a hospital in early labor increases the chance of having medications to speed up your labor or a caesarean section.

Strength could be said to be the emotional or mental qualities necessary in dealing with situations or events that are stressful or difficult. Strength isn't the display of your muscularity or your prowess; it is the power to create stability within difficult situations, holding it together until you have it together. That is strength. It deals with managing your emotions, having the right mindset as well as managing the sensations of pain.

You need strength when pushing. Even though some believe that a mom should push when she feels the sensations and overwhelming need to push, not purely when she is told the time is now. Either way, strength is needed in the delivery stage. How can you get this strength? By asking GOD for help!

Sometimes, strength will come from the presence of GOD, your spouse, knowing that he supports you and from within. Tap into that strength. Ina May Gaskin, a birthing professional in the U.S, says *"you should not let the uterus do the work in labor and birth. Fundamentally, the uterus is very strong and will be contracting to push the baby down"*. In fulfilling GOD's purpose in your life, you'll need His strength and your inner strength also.

"the Lord is our strength, all the help you need is in Him."

Strength can also come in the form of encouragement. For me, some spiritual characteristics which I have developed over time to help me survive was laid on the foundation of determination and strength from within. I was determined to make it at all costs. I made up in my mind that it was not about my condition, but rather about my decision to be successful, to be healthy, to be whole, and to be valuable. I wanted it and I wasn't giving up. I did struggle and go through pains also, but GOD helped me. It was a good thing because he placed the right people in my life to give words of encouragement or that advice which could get me over that hump in my life.

Reassurance, encouragement and reinforcement are needed in the birthing process. Labor can be a very frightening experience for moms, especially when the child is your first. How can you help women in the birthing process? Women can be helped with this by receiving adequate care, timely information, comfort, support and reassurance during labor and birth.

Reassurance is the action of removing someone's doubts or fears. If you are experiencing doubt regarding other life decisions, seek help. It may be your first time starting a business or beginning something you have never done before. This is a great time to take the advice and hear GOD's word from Proverbs 3:6, *"In all thy ways acknowledge the Lord and he will direct thy path.* In this, there is no reason for doubt and fear in the labor room.

Reassurance could come from anywhere, just like help, strength and love. But it works perfectly when it comes from someone so close to you. Reassurance helps you to be relaxed as much as possible. And just like strength, you can receive reassurance from GOD, from within, and from family and friends. The aim is to erase doubt and fears, which can be very detrimental to the birth process.

GOD is love. Love and purpose are intrinsically linked. Purpose is motivated from within or from GOD. In fact, the conception leading to birth, hopefully, is an act of love. We all know that most parents look forward to welcoming their new family member in love. Biologically, it is stated that love is meant to accompany birth. During love-making, a hormone called "oxytocin" is released and during the birthing process, it fosters feelings of love to ensure what we know as "postnatal bonding." The love existing between the mother and child is so great that it stands at number one in the hierarchy of human love, Although GOD's love is the greatest of all. Have you ever been in a labor room? The love which radiates there is incomparable. The feeling experienced by the newborn in his/her mother's arms, that love is tangible. I have been there, and I have experienced it. During labor, the labor pains of a woman may be intolerable. However, if the woman is reminded of the purpose, that little bundle of love transforms the experience. Birth could now become "optimal" or could be "a flow experience" just the way Mihaly Csikszentmihalyi calls it. The loving hand of your spouse, his encouraging words, his anticipatory looks and the care you receive from the doctor is more than enough love to carry you through all the hurdles of childbirth. We need more of this love, but it comes from within.

Strength, reassurance and love come from the inside. Love encompasses all and will provide strength and reassurance. For the love of Christ is greater than any other. Bathe yourself in the love of Christ during labor. Say to yourself. *"GOD loves me; my husband loves me; I am GOD's love; I love my child."* These statements relieve our pains.

If you love GOD, you will obey his commands. In the ministry GOD has placed you, GOD's love holds it together. No matter how ordinary you think this verse sounds, it has a strong effect on the spiritual life.

CHAPTER 10

Help Me Properly Communicate the Vision

Learning to properly communicate your thoughts and knowledge with others are very important to the success of your everyday life. When you are preparing to deliver purpose, it is crucial that you can properly communicate to those who are there to assist you. Being in leadership for over twenty-five years and working with people from all walks of life, I have found out that knowing how to communicate your visions and goals to others are crucial in obtaining success. If you are a leader and want to achieve a goal, you must be clear about what you want first. Once you have clarity, then it is important that you develop a plan of action to achieve your goals. After you have a plan of action in place, it is important to scout the right team of people to help you execute your plan. Now this is a phase where some leaders struggle because they have not developed the proper people skills to properly communicate to others.

Communication remains the most vital means of expressing yourself to others. It is the sending and receiving of information, news, ideas, feelings, visions and goals from one end to another. When you learn to communicate with people in a way that makes them value themselves, they also learn to value you. If you want to witness achieving your goals in life, learn to communicate with others in a respectful manner.

We all know that communication is not complete without the *feedback of a response*. Looking at the structure of the world now, man has invested so much time in communication. Making the world a global village, from the telephone in your hands to using a computer anywhere in the world, you literally have the world at your fingertips. When living in a world where communicating through technology is more prevalent than face-to-face interactions, we as humans can sometimes lose our way and our sense of awareness in how we are conveying messages to others. Therefore, as a leader we should work to be conscious as to how we are relaying messages to those who are there to help us achieve our purpose. I have learned as you reach certain trimesters in ministry or business, you will eventually face some communication complications. In every organization, communication problems can show up and disrupt the flow and progress of a team effort. Don't think the church has a special immunity against this. For example, notice a trail of conversation between worship leaders and volunteers.

"I didn't know we were supposed to be at rehearsal at 4:15p.m."

"We changed the rehearsal time? No one told me."

"I'm going to take the next month off it doesn't seem like you really need me anyway."

"Why did we change that song to C? We always play it in G."

Or you may have thought of these responses to those conversations as a worship leader:

"I announced the new practice time at our meeting last month."

"Does anyone even read their Planning Center e-mails?"

"Why aren't my people committed?"

"Isn't it obvious that we have to change keys with different singers sometimes?"

After reading this conversation, you can see that there was a disruption in communication. How many times have you found yourself experiencing miscommunication about something? Have you ever assumed something, and your assumption turned out to be wrong? We see from the above example that assumptions can stifle the progress of us executing our goals in ministry and business. Therefore, as a leader we should make sure we are communicating in ways that promote positive outcomes. Assumptions can really hurt relationships. Once relationships are injured, vulnerabilities in its structure begin to erode trust. Look at the business side, we can see without any exceptions, several instances where a project deadline was not met, stockholders were not well-informed about the status of the business, or a customer complaint was not handled properly. We all know that there could exist some extenuating circumstances which could cause the glitch, but we know that they could also be linked to poor or inadequate communication.

Good communication exists when the intended message you send is received by the hearer. This applies to personal communication with friends, relatives, co-workers as well. What remains very important here is CLARITY. Talking to others could be a very big problem for us. Fear of the audience reaction could play a part of the problem. But understand good communication is a part of the solution. The fact remains that a problem shared is only half solved. Remember good communication is an exchange, it's not one sided. Both parties must be able to send and receive messages.

A business is made of several teams. Effective communication among and between these teams helps get the job done well, on time and on budget. The team member who can communicate the objectives, reasoning and stepwise tasks in a very concise and coherent manner contributes greatly to the company's success.

Communicators are highly valued in today's complex and competitive business world. They are often earmarked for promotion as well as increased responsibility. The communication flow should be controlled properly, and the cross-cultural communication should also be taken into consideration. Keeping it simple is the goal of a good business communicator. When it is simple, it becomes easy to understand or comprehend. Feedback becomes effective and proper. You must have noticed that when you are preparing a document, speech or a presentation which would in turn be a game-changer for the company, simple and concise language rules over obtuse or hard to understand communication.

Who Can I Talk To and Who can I Trust?

When it comes to personal communication, we must be very wise. Telling the wrong person could do more harm than good. When asked the simple question *"Who can you talk to about your issues?"* Here are some responses:

Parents are always a good choice. They love us and the only thing they want for their children is to be happy. Maybe we can think that they won't understand us, or that they'll get angry or something, but I can say they listened to me and they made their best effort to help me. Even if they don't understand the full situation, I usually feel better, loved, listened to, and sometimes it's just what I need to keep going.

Another says: *I can talk to trusted friends and family members. If I were religious another option would be people present in the congregation, like a pastor. I could also use several sites to find active listeners who would hear what I have to say and be there for me.*

For me, there are plenty of people I could talk to. My family and friends, girlfriend or boyfriend, husband, wife, professionals, and support groups which could be live or online. It is up to me to make my choice.

From my findings, people rarely say this:

I can talk to GOD first before any other person.

The answer sounds different, doesn't it? How many of us really consult GOD? Do we really talk to GOD about our issues? Prayer has served as the conduit for communication between GOD and man. How often do we pray? How often do we table our issues at His feet? The most surprising thing is that we fail to recognize that GOD is interested in our day-to-day affairs. He wants us to trust Him for everything and anything. We should not pray only when things are going wrong, but we should always pray. It is important to say in constant communication with our Father.

What does GOD desire? How can you know GOD's mind? Both of those questions can be answered by, PRAYER!

Allow me to get personal here and tell you about an experience I had when I reached rock bottom and GOD saved me when I asked Him for help. My success didn't happen overnight; it was a process. I decided to cry out for help, when I realized that I was experiencing a spiritual miscarriage.

The two individuals I communicated to were men of GOD. They had already proven themselves to be trustworthy over time. GOD knew exactly who to have in position to bring me aide at one of the most critical times of my life. When you are directed by GOD, you must learn to trust the process. Who can you talk to about your issues? Number one GOD. Put Him first. He deserves it. No one should take that spot from Him; not your family member, your friend, not your co-worker and not even your pastor. Talk to GOD concerning everything pertaining to you, your personal life, family life, spiritual life, business life and public life. I promise GOD will send what you need at the right time.

When we decide to *leave GOD out of it*, we face trust issues, not knowing who to trust. What is trust? Trust could be said to be the acceptance of the **truth** of a statement without **evidence or investigation**. You just believe; you don't need to validate such a belief. That is trust!

One day, I came across a portion of the Bible, this part got me thinking, maybe because I interpreted it solely. I brought out this verse and pondered on it alone without reading the chapter through: *Do not trust a neighbor; put no confidence in a friend. Even with her who lies in your embrace be careful of your words*[55]. I could remember my train of thought first. I understood that GOD was a jealous GOD, but was He telling us to trust Him and Him alone? I thought of the *'her'* who lies in my embrace-my wife. Was He saying that I shouldn't trust her too? No! GOD wasn't saying that. He was only making it clear to us that man would fail us. If you look at that chapter, He was talking about the Misery of Israel. In verse 2 it says: *The Godly have been swept from the land; not one upright man remains.* **You can't trust the unrighteous.**

The Bible says that they are governed by the flesh. Who can you trust? GOD and GOD alone. This doesn't mean that we can't trust others naturally like our family members and close friends, people who have been with us through thick and thin, friends whose

---

[55] Micah 7: 5 (NIV).

relationship stood the test of time and difficulty. We can trust them. A pregnant woman has to her support team wisely because she should trust the doctor to do his best, the nurse, and the health services the clinic offers. Although, just like any patient, she has the privilege to change doctors. E. M Forster says, *"One must be fond of people and trust them if one is not to make a mess of life."*

Lord, Receive Me Or Love Me Again; Remind Me Why You Chose Me And Loved Me For This Baby.

This should be more of a prayer than a topic for discussion.

Lord, remind me why you chose me and loved me for who I am in you. You could possibly take another one.

JOHN 15:16

The above passage established the fact that you did not choose GOD-He chose you for His will. We have discussed how being pregnant with GOD's purpose and the fact that He partnered with us to make this baby shows that GOD has been involved since day one. In fact, He has anointed us for his purpose. *'For the Spirit of the Sovereign LORD is on me, because the LORD has anointed me to preach good news to the poor. He has sent me to bind up the brokenhearted, to proclaim freedom for the captives and release from darkness for the prisoners. . ."*[56]

---

[56] Isaiah 61:1

The question on your lips now might be: *Why did He choose me? Why not somebody else?* Well, He chose you because He is GOD.

Your mistake and mishaps don't scare Him. Romans 8: 14-15 talks about being adopted into GOD's family. GOD has adopted us. He has chosen to love us and that is why He gave us His Son JESUS Christ. He chose us for His will and that is why He created us. Hebrews 4:16 tells us that we have access to GOD. Some of us think that GOD is just angry in the distance, just waiting to judge you and hand out His divine smack-down on you. You have gotten it all wrong. He is our Lord and King, and He chose us for this "Baby." During delivery or birthing, we should call on Him to remind us of His plans for us and with us.

CHAPTER ELEVEN

I Can Do This

Seeing through the challenges that have been elucidated more about in the previous chapters, there can still be this doubt lurking somewhere in your heart about your capability of giving birth and probably parenting the baby. This can be likened to a doubt of the potentials, ideas that won't only bring that business of yours to reality but also drag it to the limelight. My grandfather taught me great lessons of faith to use, when fear tries to creep in my spirit. He said; 'the fact that you do not see a way does not mean that there is no way. He would continue saying, while you are trying to figure it out, GOD has already worked it out!" Then he would finish his statement by having me turn to Proverbs 3:5-6 and read it out loud.

"Trust in the Lord with all thy heart and lean not to thy own understanding and in all thy ways acknowledge the Lord and he will direct thy path."

A wavering man receives nothing from the Lord. Circumstances around you may be against your dreams. It may be the system of government of the day, government policies, financial constraints, geographical location, acceptability from friends, family, intimidation, etc. There are situations that can warrant and necessitate a miscarriage. So, let your attention not be drawn to the impossibilities but fixed on the possibility and actualization of the desired result. You should allay yourself of the fears attached to the conception of the successful birth of the business, ministry, developing ideas, etc.

A miscarriage can be caused by your worries and concerns about the safe delivery of the baby. This can bring about psychological imbalance for the expectant mother and thus endangers the survival of the fetus. So many dreams and ideas have been terminated untimely as a result of constantly focusing on the little percentage of an impossibility rate. You may say to yourself, 'I can no longer go forward in the pursuance of this. I think at this point, I should give up.' Giving up should not be an option. Don't be held down by those fears and worries at the near-success-point. Encourage yourself in the Lord and focus on the positive.

"The thought I have towards you is of good and not of evil.

<u>To give you an expected end</u>.[57]"

This is not to add to the causes of miscarriage in chapter 4, but to let you know that amidst all odds, 'YOU CAN DO THIS'. Whisper to

---

[57] *Jeremiah 29:11*

yourself: I can! I can do all things through Christ that strengthens me! Believe that you can surmount the insurmountable. In the words of Napoleon Hills, he said; *"whatever the mind of man can believe and conceive, it can definitely achieve."*

The power behind the conception and belief will intermittently make things work. It is not for you to think negative of, but for you to manifest the purpose that is being nurtured in the womb of your heart. When you wake up every day, declare the positive things that you want to come to pass. The Bible says, *"They call those things that were not as if they were.*[58]*"* That is an exercise of faith. Yes! When the confession is made, everything you are trying to do, accomplish and acquire is compelled to you and favor is released. "Everything" must respect you because you are meant to dominate and make nature and conditions your subject. Man, at creation, was created to dominate over the fishes of the sea and other animals of the earth. Thusly making man a ruler over circumstances and forces of nature and not subject to them.

It isn't good for people to continue to wallow in complaints and worries about how bad things seem against the accomplishments of their business or ministry intent. I've met with some leaders over the years in business and in ministry. There have been those who work towards with positive attitude and had a successful outcome. Other had a very negative outlook, after they

---

[58] Romans 4:17

did their calculations and presented their arguments, the next thing that would come up was the language of backing out. This is how years of prayer and hard work can be delayed. Therefore, surround yourself with leaders and team-members who can see a positive way to help achieve your purpose.

Protect Your Baby

Protect Your Baby

The people who you share your ideas with also matters a lot. Discouragement from friends can also bring about doubt. Comments like: What a stupid idea! That's ridiculous! I'll quit if I were you! These negative statements will not only make you sway the realization of the idea but also doubt your purpose. It's not everyone that you should share your intentions with. For the growth of the idea that you've conceived, what is required is sharing with like minds, so that the nourishment of the idea can blossom in faith.

In a conversation with Tom, a manager of a paper producing company, he expressed how displeased he was with his employment. He complained about the pay and the working hours. 'Despite all the hours I spend working tirelessly for the company, they pay me peanuts in return.' he said angrily. Tom shared the story of his friend not working as much as he does but earns better than him. All through the conversation I was able to sense that Tom was worried because of the unhealthy comparison he nursed in his heart. He was comparing his life to that of his friend's.

Comparison is not good for the health of anything and a purported act of folly. Little wonder why the Bible expressed that, *"We wouldn't put ourselves in the same class with or compare ourselves to those who are bold enough to make their own recommendations. Certainly, when they measure themselves by themselves and compare themselves to themselves, they show how foolish they are."*

You should not compare the lucrative tendencies of your business ideas with that of your friend's. You should not compare the growth of some existing church ministries to yours not minding the variables (everyone is given according to its own ability).

Everyone Doesn't Respond The Same

According to medical experts in the dispensing of drugs, the likely reaction to the drug(s) differs. That is why usage should be prescription based and on the doctor's diagnosis after carrying out a series of medical tests. Again, because the side effects of a drug may differ from person to person.

Even twins birthed on the same day may not have the same purpose and level of grace. Always note that you are different from others and never bank on comparisons. This doesn't allow the growth and development of the fetus but will abruptly put an end to the vision and the promising ideas within. Constantly comparing yourself to others can cause you to end up being frustrated when you compare your inputs and results with that of others you deem more successful than you.

The help needed for a safe delivery may not be ultimately rendered by the experts consulted but by the one whose ultimate help supersedes that of men or apparatuses employed. Few years ago, while walking along the streets of New York City, I sighted a pregnant lady. From all indications and the size of her tummy, the pregnancy should not have been less than five months. She appeared weak and helpless. What popped in to my mind, was the fact that she could not help herself out and this called for the help of others.

If GOD can give the assurance that He will answer us in the days of trouble, I see no reason why we should hesitate to run to him for the help that can transform our life, career, business, or ministry. When we seek refuge from GOD before it is too late, GOD can prevent the foreseen and perceived miscarriages we could have had. GOD created everyone with a purpose and this purpose is to be executed with His help. Going back to the author of the purpose is like going back to get the architecture design on paper, when there is a problem in the construction of the building. He's got the architecture design of your purpose with him and he can fix it when there is an error, that is if you just get back to the source.

There's More To Me

A human life is sometimes characterized by aspirations. The ambitious man is one who works with the expectations of getting results. These results are referred to as goals and ambitions. All of us have ambition, what's interesting is the striking difference in them. The goal of an expectant mother is to give birth to the awaited baby. That of the businessman is getting more profits. The aim of someone who is works in ministry is to touch lives and impact souls. In order to achieve the different objectives and reach the pinnacle of success; one must seek out the appropriate approach and aim individually. For instance, a business man/woman's approach to making profits, may be getting new customers which can be done in a positive or the negative way. They may choose to improve the quality of products and services rendered or tarnish the image of other existing businesses through nefarious acts just to gain more customers.

Also, for someone who wants to be a minister, touching lives and impacting destinies. The approach may be either to create outreach programs or meet financial needs of people around as well as preaching the message of hope and salvation.

The actualization of a conceived dream, vision and idea is great. But there is more to it beyond what is expected. Just like the feeling of accomplishment after birth, the baby's mother basks in the euphoria of the new child for some time and then eventually realizes that there is more to life than just giving birth. Don't misinterpret this. One of the purposes that The Lord gave mankind at creation was procreation which was termed as 'multiplication and fruitfulness'[59] in the Bible.

This procreation is not restricted to child births alone. You are meant to yield fruits from your business ideas as well. Also, you are meant to multiply in your vision for the ministry or calling. But that is not all. All things are meant to be for the glory of the Lord.

As a matter of fact, all gifts, ideas, visions and dreams are meant to be concerted towards glorifying The Lord amidst men. Hannah prayed earnestly at Shiloh for a child after a long time of waiting. She could no longer endure the mockery attached to being barren. She asked for the boy Samuel with a promise to bring back the child for GOD's service with the purpose of fulfilling the utmost goal of mankind to GOD. If she had done otherwise, the Lord might not even consider making Samuel the next priest of Israel and blessing her with the other children that Hannah was able to give birth to.[60] Giving the glory to GOD goes beyond and above what we can bargain for. It guarantees the security of the idea and the rapid growth of it.

Our business or Ministry is not meant for self-glory but for GOD's glory. We shouldn't see the results as a product of our work alone, like some people do. They go about saying 'I', 'I', 'I', in all events boasting about what they were able to achieve (through the help of GOD). This boastful nature negates the principle of giving the glory back to GOD. Like we've highlighted in the previous

---

[59] Genesis 1:28
[60] I Samuel 1 & 2

paragraphs, many people have spoilt their good ideas with selfish interests. Ministries have crumbled because of self-aggrandizement. When the purpose of something is misplaced, the abuse of such will be inevitable.

Some at the end of the day won't reach the apex because of the quest to solely amass wealth which is against the initial purpose of the dream at conception. They reckoned with GOD's purpose at the infancy of that business idea or ministry intent but when there was a little growth, they deviated from the purpose of GOD as in regards their visions and aspirations.

The benefits humanity derives from the birth also matters a lot. When a child is born, the little baby is not meant to only brighten the face of the parents but also brings joy to the entire human community. This is as a result of the plus in the population of the people in the society. Whatever business or ideas to be worked on, one of the primal aims should be to benefit the society by either relieving her of a burden or creating a solution to her problem.

Social vices and some societal ills have been encouraged through the birth of ideas and innovations as well. Companies that produce cigarettes make money and huge profits at the end of their business year. But instead of solving a problem, they compound the ones that exist already. The birth of an idea is important but beyond the birth, the glory that would be ascribed to GOD and the blessings that humans will enjoy is more important and laudable.

The Bible as the word of GOD is a compass and light to the path of anyone who seeks knowledge especially those whom are looking to come into alignment with GOD's purpose for their life (business idea, innovation, dreams and aspirations).

"So, can I… if others have made it through this, so can I"

Across the globe, there are so many people who have sailed through miscarriages. Daily, the birth of thousands of children that is being recorded has proven that thousands of miscarriages that ought to have occurred were prevented. The late Steve Jobs was able to create the Apple empire because of his nursed love for electronics even when he was a kid. Young Jobs felt he should do well in the humanities and arts, but he was pregnant with the idea to build something electrical. Do you love something passionately? Do you have the keen interest to venture into a business or ministry? You can go for it! If late Jobs' idea could survive miscarriage, yours won't be an exception.

Another example is Thomas Edison who invented the bulb. After several attempts to illuminate through the bulb, Edison was able to come up with what we all use for illumination now. With ninety-nine failed attempts to get the desired result, Edison had more than ninety-nine reasons to give up, but he didn't. He strove hard till he was able achieve his aim. There was a 99% likelihood of a miscarriage, but he did not give in to the challenges. In an interview with Edison on his success, he made it known that he has learnt ninety-nine ways a bulb can't produce light. That is someone who has tried so many times but saw the failed trials as a challenge towards the fulfillment of his dream of illuminating the world electrically.

Have you ever failed in the pursuance of your dreams? Are you being faced with the difficulties and impossibilities? Don't stop trying today. Maybe the next trial is what the world is waiting for (that great invention or innovation of yours). If Edison could surmount the challenges attached to failed attempts, you can as well.

Let's check some of the biblical instances too. David with the potential to rule his people, was limited in terms of geographical position. Meanwhile, instead of living with the right people who will help in the actualization of his dreams, he was just a shepherd boy in the wilderness. By human reasoning, David was far from the manifestations of his ideas. But the most striking significance of his story is that he wasn't idle in the wilderness. Rather than sulking and murmuring about how bad everything was against or making negative confessions against his life and destiny, David took care of the sheep with diligence. After saving the life of a lamb by devouring the bear. I can imagine the heavens saying, "this is the right man for the job". He had several encounters in the bush and he remained strong and undaunted in his pursuit of his dreams. He did not relent because of hard times and situations that could lead to miscarriages or even abortion of the business ideas, ministry intent and dreams.

When Goliath was boasting and bragging to the Israelites, they were jittering for forty days and no one could confront the philistines that were defiling the Almighty GOD. The so called heavily built brothers of David could not rise to the challenge. The burning desire of young David to defend his GOD was what could not make him leave the scene when he was sent as the errand boy to go and feed his brothers at the war front.

" "

~ Daniel 11:32

Before David fought, he diminished the power of the 'uncircumcised philistine' and claimed victory. His victory was not a surprise to me because he conceived the victory and believed that it will surely come to pass.

"You shall decree a thing and it shall be established."

~ Job 22:28

He didn't panic or confess defeat like some would do if they were in such a situation. That was why he was able to do exploits with just five stones and a sling. Ordinarily, those apparatuses can't bring down a giant of Goliath's standing, but the enemy fell as a result of the involvement of GOD's help in the battle.

One with GOD Is a Majority

This could be accepted spiritually and even literarily. You may be the only one standing on your stance about your beliefs, while others are set to discourage you; but one thing is for sure, whoever is on the Lord's side cannot be put to shame. You are not alone, GOD is with you. You must have heard from others several times, how they walked the path no one has ever treaded because of their inner conviction. If GOD is with you, it becomes easy.

Are you planning to back out after you've considered your positioning and the rejection from people? Don't! David was able to defeat the enemy of his people and that marked the beginning of his greatness. It led him to the throne at the end and David was one of the greatest Kings of Israel. If David can, nothing should stop you from birthing your ideas and dreams.

Joseph as a case study is a replica of someone who made it against all challenges. As the son of the aged Jacob, he was loved by his father, while being the son of his old age. Joseph was despised greatly by his brothers, who saw the preferential treatment given by their father to him. As an object of jealousy coupled with the dreams of Joseph to rule over all, only intensified their hate for him. One of the most hurtful enemies one can dare have is enemies among kindred. These enemies are deadlier because they virtually know all your of strengths and weaknesses. They can easily harness the opportunity to inflict pain just like the case of Joseph.

In the land of Egypt, where he was sold to the house of Potiphar, Joseph was diligent in the discharge of his duties and that earned him the position of head servant. The poor boy didn't see that as the peak of his career unlike people who get blinded after little success attained. He didn't lose focus when the wife of his master, wanted to lure him to her bed. You know what? Joseph fled knowing fully the plans of GOD for his life. He refused to soil his destiny at the altar of adultery.

The good deed of Joseph avoiding the defilement of the bed of his master was reciprocated with his arrest and detainment in prison. But even in the prison, Joseph was not discouraged. He did not murmur against GOD, like some will resort to. 'GOD saw me going through hell in my business and was silent'- *they will grumble*. Joseph with his charisma was made the controller of the prison. Try imagining a prisoner being made a controller of the prison. Joseph was the boss even in the prison. Guess what? Joseph ended up ruling as the prime minister in a foreign land. This should make you understand that a bend in the road is not the end of the road.

Joseph faced three 'P's before he was able to become an achiever –

1. He was thrown into the [**P**]**it** by his brothers,
2. Sold to into slavery, bought by [**P**]otiphar's house,
3. thrown into the [P]rison for an act he knew nothing about.

In the end, Joseph ended up with the two 'P's of his dreams

1. He was eventually made the [**P**]rime minister
2. Lived in the [**P**]**alace** thereafter.

Considering the rigorous and demanding challenges Joseph faced, he should have just told himself;' let me sleep with my master's wife and secure a place for myself in the house of Potiphar'.

But he did not because that could have aborted the long-time-conceived dream and ended up living as a failure with shattered dreams and goals.

Joseph combated those challenges and he sailed through. If he could sail through the enemies of his father's house; if he was able to overcome the seduction of his master's wife at the expense of his freedom; then you can also bring that dream of yours to manifestation regardless of the negative circumstances surrounding it.

"Wherefore seeing we also are compassed about with so great a cloud of witnesses, let us lay aside every weight, and the sin which doth so easily beset us, and let us run with patience the race that is set before us. ~Hebrews: 12:1"

Having given examples of people who came, saw and conquered; you are not expected to think of yourself as a failure or even, mediocre because you have what it takes to achieve greatness. Of all the cases we studied, there are some attributes and character straits they all share:

1. The will to overcome their numerous challenges was present in their approaches.
2. They weren't just satisfied with the average level of attainment.
3. They pursued their course with resilience and perseverance.

It's not for you as a "go getter" to consider giving up. The race may be tough, and the journey may not be easy but just as we were able to learn from David's and Joseph's instances; we have a responsibility to maintain and reaffirm our determination for success. More importantly, in all their biddings, they didn't rule out "the GOD factor". They didn't go against the laws of the Lord because of the unending love and fear they had for GOD and his commandments. They didn't want to go against the tenets of GOD. What any other person would have considered as an opportunity for fun, Joseph called it a sin against GOD and his master. Instead of enjoying the bosom of his master's wife, he fled. Learn to flee from all appearances of evil.

David on the other hand couldn't stand Goliath defiling the army of the Lord with derogatory words. He swung to action because of his passion to the service of the Lord.

In order to be helped against miscarriages, such visionary must be a GOD lover. Sin should be a no-go-area for that person. You can't live in sin and at the same moment live in accordance with GOD's purpose. Remember, it is our ordinary plus GOD's extra, that creates the extraordinary.

'Let us therefore run the race with patience'.

Like the common saying- *'Rome wasn't built in a day'*, growth is a step by step process. You may not have arrived at the desired destination of your dreams today but remain faithful. Exercising diligence and patience will get you there. Therefore, you should not be in a hurry, as for GOD's plan for your life- it is systematic and strategic. The fact that you are still here now says you are a part of a bigger plan and you will get to your destiny in GOD's own timing.

"There is time for everything under the sun."

Allow me to reinforcement the essence of this chapter: If we can practice being patient without comparing ourselves with others, progression in our business or ministry will be remarkable. This principle causes us to become better than what we used to be, rather than striving to be better than anyone else.

CHAPTER TWELVE

I Won't Let GOD Down

Your purpose in life is to fulfill GOD's plan for humanity. This plan is to impact lives in such a way that it warrants them to give all the glory back to GOD. This is what you are created for! Many times, people derail from this plan and they do otherwise. They do this in the pursuit of their own personal agendas and respective dreams. Whatever is not giving glory to GOD is against GOD's initial plan for mankind.

Larry and his friends after college intended to start a drug business to make money. They started the business after putting so many things in place. The business transactions yielded profits, and this gave them the ability to live a luxurious life. They would go about drinking, clubbing and partying without a sense of purpose. They were running after the wrong things in life and headed down a road of destruction. I was privileged to meet Larry in a supermarket, and I shared the gospel of JESUS Christ with him. Larry in response to my preaching, said emphatically that he didn't need JESUS. Of course, he had everything- money, connection, luxuries... at his beck and call. I guess this illegal business really supplemented his lifestyle but kept him on a dangerous road of mischief.

Two years later, I was ministering at a yearly prison outreach, I bumped into Larry. His face looked haggard, but I could recognize him. In our one-hour long conversation, he told me about the apprehension of his group which led to the death of three of his friends. He stated, "The police came after us that night. They fired gunshots at us and in the process, the other three died and I was left to face the wrath of the law. I was sentenced to five years imprisonment and this is just the first year.' He said as he sobbed with a shrill cry." I felt a kind of compassion towards this young man. I understood his plight and introduced JESUS to him again. He gave his life to JESUS and surrendered his heart totally to GOD. I gave him one of the bibles I had on me and told him about the ineffable love of Christ towards him. 'GOD is ready to give you a new beginning and make all your crooked ways straight.' I assured him.

Years had passed, and I was invited to be the keynote speaker at a conference. When I arrived inside of the building I was met by Larry, smiling alongside a pretty lady. They also came for the conference and guess what? Larry was one of the guest preliminary testimonial speakers. Larry shared how GOD transformed his life beyond the four walls of prison and how GOD used me to help walk him through the call to Salvation. Larry is currently a senior pastor and happily married with three children.

GOD has given men the freedom to make some decisions even when he knows what is right for us.

"He said here lies before you light and darkness, life and death choose for yourself one." ~ Deuteronomy 30:15

Man is at liberty to make so many choices that will make or mar him, his ideas, his dreams and visions. This makes man directly responsible for his choices. GOD is all powerful and regarded as 'omnipotent' but there are myriads of things that He restrains himself from, allowing man to make and live with the consequences of his decisions.

Yes! The Bible affirms that *"With GOD all things are possible."*[61] In Him, there is no impossibility. There are some things that He can do but He won't do. GOD will try convincing you by sending people to you, to make you turn away from your sinful ways. He sent me to Larry, but he refused at the first encounter in the supermarket. GOD's will was not forced on him that is why the Bible says, *'The gift of GOD that brings salvation as appeared to all men.'*[62]

If Larry had chosen not to accept Christ even at the meeting in the prison, he probably would have ended up without Christ. GOD expressed in the book of Revelation that, *'Behold I stand at the door knocking and if anyone hears my voice and opens the door,*

---

[61] Matthew 19:26
[62] Titus 2:11

I'll come in and dine with him."[63] He has the power to break the door instead of knocking but the amazing thing is that, He won't. He cherishes the Agape love and not love out of compulsion. It's just an expression of love from Him.

Looking at the terrain of events, many people believe that purpose is all about living a life of comfort and luxury but it's beyond that. Though Larry was able to achieve that, however the way he got it was not in line with the will of GOD for his life. And it wasn't all what GOD had in store for him. The scripture states "*… all things are working together for the good of them that love GOD and who are called according to **His purpose**."*[64]

GOD's purpose gives us life. Whether you are in leadership, a parent, teacher or a new believer; GOD wants to give you "life" and that more abundantly.

In business, when you're in line with GOD's plan, everything tends to fall into place to your advantage. It will be a surprise to the heathen and unbeliever that you are still succeeding, irrespective of the harsh government policies, unfavorable balance of payment and economic downsizing. It's all about it being a subset of GOD's plan. In ministry work, your growth tends to be a wonder to fellow men considering your location and challenges. *"Faithful is he who calls you, who is able to bring it to pass."* [65]

---

[63] Revelation 3:20
[64] Romans 8:28
[65] 1 Thessalonians 5:24

Even if you are considered a "new-comer" with little to no resources to contributed to the development of that idea, you will end up getting an awesome result. Not because it's magical but because you have centered your plans and ideas around GOD's purpose. We might derail from the purpose of GOD at times, but the Lord is merciful and kind to help get us back on track. Don't wait until you learn it the hard way. You are a masterpiece of GOD. Fashion your visions to suit GOD's purpose and the result will be marvelous.

I have chatted with some people and after listening to the gospel of JESUS Christ, they will come up with questions like, "Can He really save me, despite my ugly pasts? Can He truly make my sins white as snow like you claimed?" Apparently Yes! There is no transgression that is beyond GOD's forgiveness. That's what the Bible refers to stating that; *"all have sinned and fall short of the glory of the Lord."*[66] If one is willing to repent and forsake his/her sinful ways, GOD is able and just to forgive our sins and give us a new beginning.

In order to retrace your steps back to the one who has the architectural designs for your life, in his custody, first and foremost, there should be a sense of realization. A problem cannot be solved if it's not acknowledged. Larry, as earlier mentioned, received salvation when he realized that he needed a solution; unlike his

---

[66] Romans 3:23

disposition years ago at the supermarket. It is easier to combat challenges after the realizing stage.

Afterwards, the next is confession. There is power in confession because the power of the tongue, over all the other parts of the body can't be underestimated. We need to confess, profess and accept, that GOD is the author of our purpose in life. During this process, what is paramount is that you believe in GOD's power to save and grant you help that is found wanting in your life. This belief will reflect in your confession. What follows confession?

Repentance! You must learn to forsake the old, unfruitful ways of your life. This can result in the abandonment of former pursuits that were against the purpose of GOD. Sometimes, many things can be jeopardized at this stage just to cling to the will of the "Author" friends, connection, luxuries and what have we. It doesn't end there because the Bible urges us to work out *'our own soul salvation with fear and trembling'.*[67] It should be a daily exercise which can be achieved through prayer and studying of the scriptures in order to be approved of GOD. Living a life that is fashioned and in alignment with the ultimate purpose of GOD, is the "**good life**". We were created for this!

---

[67] Philippians 2:12

CHAPTER THIRTEEN

I Am What I Am by The Grace of GOD

"The very center and core of the whole Bible is the doctrine of the grace of GOD."

-J. Gresham Machen

Yes, **grace** has been one of the most important concepts in the Bible, in Christianity and in the world. Buswell writes: *"The goodness of GOD in this sense-that is, the grace of GOD-is the most amazing theme in all the Bible."* The most astounding truth ever proclaimed is that GOD is and remains absolutely just and at the same time, He justifies-He makes just and right those who are unjust, unrighteous, guilty and defiled," It is clearly expressed in the promises of GOD which has been revealed in the scripture and personified in JESUS Christ. What is grace? The love of GOD shown to the unlovely and undeserving world. Grace is something that GOD gives us that none of us deserves. It is the peace of GOD given to the restless and the unwarranted favor of GOD. Some people have defined grace in some special ways;

"Grace is free sovereign favor to the ill-deserving." B.B. Warfield

"Grace is love that cares and stoops and rescues." John Scott

"Grace is GOD reaching downward to people who are in rebellion against Him." Jerry Bridges

"Grace is unconditional love toward a person who does not deserve it." Paul Zahl.

The most surprising thing about grace is that everyone desperately needs it, but it's not about us. Grace is primarily a *word* about GOD. According to Michael Horton-"In grace, GOD gives nothing less than Himself-Grace, then, is not a third thing or substance mediating between GOD and sinners but is JESUS Christ in redeeming action". As Christians we live every day by the grace of GOD. The root of forgiveness is found in GOD's endless riches shown to us through grace. Paul tells us that, "the grace of GOD has appeared, bringing salvation for all people, training us to renounce ungodliness and worldly passions, and to live self-controlled, upright, and Godly lives".[68] Spiritual growth never happens overnight; we grow in the grace and the knowledge of our Lord and Savior JESUS Christ.

---

[68] Titus 2:11

Grace is the basis for the following:

- ✓ The Christian identity
- ✓ It is also the basis for our standing before GOD.
- ✓ It is also our living.
- ✓ It is our strength for living.
- ✓ It is our Power to succeed, in life, ministry and business!

CHAPTER FOURTEEN

The Challenge of Birthing A Blessing

Early in the year 2005, Union Spring was operating with hardly any money. We were struggling to pay for the life center that we had built in 1998. I wasn't even receiving a salary due to all the debt. It was such a bad time for the church. The officers and deacons blamed me for the position we were in financially. I was mentally and emotionally drained because I wanted everything to work out. In my spirit I knew I could count on GOD and that a plan of victory was in motion, but I didn't know how GOD was going to get us out of this. So, I prayed, and I encouraged our leaders to pray and believe GOD.

Months passed and in late August of 2005, Hurricane Katrina wreaked havoc in the state of Louisiana. I began to pray for the people of the city of New Orleans and surrounding areas that were being affected by this terrible storm. GOD spoke to me and told me to open the doors of the life center to help those in need. When I presented the idea to the church, some gave negative feedback. One of the officers asked; *"How can we open the doors to the public when we can barely pay our bills?"* I responded; ***"I don't know but, GOD told me to do it"***. I opened the life center without worrying about the conditions. I had faith and made the decision to obey the voice of GOD. Being a leader sometimes you must make that last decision that can ether shift the ministry/business forward or backwards. Therefore, I encourage every leader to develop a strong relationship with GOD. Stay connected to the power source and in those times of adversity you can get clear instructions from GOD.

I decided to trust and lean on the Lord. If we ask GOD to be our Jehovah-Jireh in our lives; He must create a situation that He can be a provider in. When your decisions line up with the word of GOD, Heaven will support you. Our decisions will cause us to have to take certain actions. It was a challenge for me to trust GOD nothing was making any sense. The church was right, we didn't have the money, nor the resources to open our doors and receive the people that had been affected.

I got a call late one night asking if we could take people in because a bus from New Orleans had stopped in Mansfield. The people were hungry and wet. Some had been separated from their family members. Although, people were suffering, this was the situation that GOD created where He could prove Himself to be a provider. I called members to come help me make those people comfortable. There were several members who brought food, clothing and shoes. Then our local Sheriff assisted us with temporary sleeping beds. Then Pastors, Leaders and the community gave monetary donations, so we could properly house the displaced family. Look at GOD! Red Cross came out to help. GOD really began to bless in a big way. We had over 100 people that we took in for months. I was away from the church one day running errands, when I received a call from Sister Hensley. She said, "Pastor, there are people here at the church with a trailer full of stuff". I rushed back to the church to find my dear friend, Dr. Benjamin Lockhart, Sr. had driven a U-Haul all the way to Catuna, Louisiana from Marietta, Georgia to help. Dr. Lockhart was the Pastor of Pleasant Grove Baptist Church. GOD provided like never before. Pilots began to fly into Grand Cane, Louisiana. This rural town has a small airport not far from Catuna. Plane after plane brought in supplies, food and clothing. We were so excited and leaped with the joy of the lord because GOD showed Himself strong to all of us especially the families in need!

We went from zero to tens of thousands in our bank account because of donations from Homeland Security and the DeSoto Parish Police Jury to help keep our church running while we housed the evacuees of New Orleans. See, this is why obedience is better than sacrifice. If I would have operated out of fear and decided based on our church circumstances, we would have missed out on the opportunity assist a lot of great people. I encourage every leader to follow the leading of GOD and you shall prosper!

There will be **challenges while birthing a blessing**. I knew some way, somehow, it would happen, but I had no idea that trusting GOD would pay off like it did. Trust GOD and trust the process!

In order to give birth, you must endure pain. The struggle was great, but GOD was greater! I believe that GOD is trying to birth something right now! Never lose faith or stop trusting in GOD.

If I SURVIVED, So Can You

In 2001, I went through spiritual blockage in my life. It was August 2001, GOD spoke to me and told me not to call anyone else down to preach at our annual revival at Union Spring but to do it myself. This was during the time that I had separated from my previous wife. The church was greatly affected by the separation. Many wouldn't receive a word I said. They had built an invisible wall and blocked out the word. I needed that wall to fall because their spiritual state was in stake.

Wall: *A way of feeling or behaving that completely prevents two groups of people from communicating with or understanding each other.*

Example: A wall of mistrust between two groups.

A wall can block you from entering your promised land. The ancient city of Jericho did not want the Hebrew Nation of Israel to be its master. It shut itself up. Jericho trusted the strength of its walls to stand behind its defense and not to surrender, or desire conditions of peace. The enemy devised a plan to stop the church and Pastor from communicating. If we continued to shut each other out, the plan would prevail.

SHUT UP

Many people allow their circumstances to make them shut themselves in. They allow their past to haunt them, they don't accept change. They just shut up! We must allow ourselves to remain open for change. When you are destined for great the enemy will always try to stop you. Jericho is the first battle you must fight in order to go any further.

We must open our minds. When I began to open my mind, things begin to change. What happened in Jericho was that they had built a wall around their mind. Nothing could enter in or come out. They had encountered so much that they did not trust anyone. Walls are built to protect you from further pain. Walls are built to keep people from getting in. These walls can become like a prison. In some instances, we can unknowingly imprison ourselves. We lock ourselves in and get comfortable and later we find that it is difficult for us to break free. Don't allow anyone, including yourself to shut you out of your blessings, deliverance, healing, gifts, etc.

Living Behind The Walls

It seemed that I was living behind walls. I could clearly hear GOD speaking to me, but I couldn't be delivered because of the walls. The devil had me thinking that I had to shut myself out because of my problems. I would preach and teach my heart out and go back to hiding in sorrow behind the walls. These walls imposed immense and unnecessary suffering.

When living behind walls you lose access to many things, your children, your spouse, your world as you once knew it. No one can get close to you. Your children want to talk or play but they can't, due to the walls. You can't properly communicate with your spouse, they may feel rejected and there will be very little intimacy. These walls were ruining my life. I felt like I was losing my mind. I cried out to GOD one night asking him for "HELP"! I realized I was battling a stronghold of depression. *A stronghold is a mindset that accepts a situation as unchangeable. What happened was I had built a wall around my mind and could not escape.* I was shut up!

Living with your back against the wall

I began to get tired, I was drained. I needed rest and peace in my mind. When your back is against the wall, it symbolizes that you are weary, and needing to be rescued. I knew I had to get up. So, I got up! How did I get up? I had to remove the walls. If you are going to give birth to your purpose, you must allow GOD to turn your pain into purpose by removing the walls. In time you will see that surrendering yourself and problems to GOD will bring about the peace you need, in order to carry on into the next phase of your life.

The Struggle In The Womb

The struggle will always take place before you give birth. It starts when conception begins. In the story of Jacob & Esau[69], After Rebekah conceived the twins, the fight was on! The Bible says when she was quickened with child, before her delivery, the two children within her womb struggled with each other.

They were battling for the blessing! Jacob was the heel grabber, he wanted to be first. You must be careful whenever you get anxious and can't wait on the full process of birth. There will be uneasiness and extreme pain in the body.

Rebekah asked, "Why me?" Were things this hard with other women? Have you ever asked the question why? She felt that the pain was unbearable. She wondered if she had been too eager to conceive? All these things Rebekah inquired from the Lord. She asked the Lord for HELP!

The commotion was what our younger generation likes to call "extra". The desire for children was her trouble, now the struggle is no longer so. *"If GOD hath granted me my desire in the conception of a child, what means this disturbance and conflict within me, which threatens me with loss before I enjoy it"* Said Rebekah.

---

[69] Genesis 25:22a

Don't let the devil deceive you into devaluing this gift. There is still a blessing hidden inside the womb, even though it comes along with struggle. Sometimes, GOD's sovereignty is invisible. We can't see it while we're struggling, but it's definitely there.

Who Will You Be After This Struggle?

Two nations were battling on the inside. Jacob was determined to get out first. GOD already has a spot for you, be patient and wait on the Lord. He knows exactly what He is doing!

Help From The Midwives

GOD had some midwives in place to help. Pharaoh said to the midwives, *"I want you to kill all the sons"*[70]. The devil intended to take us out! But GOD knew Moses was coming through the line. The Lord knows you are coming down the line. Whenever GOD has something for you, He always has some premeditated arrangements. He always had a plan for your life. He will lead you in the right direction and assign someone to your life to usher you into safety. We are here now because of GOD's arrangement.

The midwives decided they would disobey Pharaoh. They spared the sons and GOD said to the midwives, "I won't forget about you." Some of you have a "Midwife's Ministry". Your job may not to be "up front", but it just might be to help someone who is. You were born to encourage others and keep them lifted up. GOD won't

---

[70] Exodus 1:15-21

forget about you. GOD will bless you for being faithful to your calling.

When you have the spirit of a midwife, you want to see others blessed. A midwife doesn't have a "hater" spirit. They believe that when GOD blesses others, the line gets shorter and blessings are coming soon for them as well.

And it came to pass, because the midwives feared GOD that He made them houses.[71] ~ This is biblical proof that GOD will bless you, when you help someone else. So, in conclusion, make a commitment not to just help yourself, but your family and those who GOD brings across your path as well.

---

[71] Exodus 1:21

CHAPTER FIFTEEN

Parental Praise

When Mary (Mother of JESUS) entered Zechariah's home greeting Elizabeth. As Elizabeth hears her greeting, her own baby leaped in her womb and she was filled with the Holy Spirit. Elizabeth explained that she knew Mary was chosen to be the mother of the Messiah by the joyous movement of her unborn child in response to Mary's greeting. [72]

When Elizabeth heard the voice, three things happened:

1. The baby (John) in in her womb leaped for joy
2. She was filled with the Holy Spirit
3. She prophesied

---

[72] *Luke 1:39-45*

Elizabeth called Mary blessed. Mary was carrying blessed fruit in her womb. *Prenatal means before birth. Praise means strong approval or admiration of.* We can give GOD "Prenatal Praise" because we know that it's coming. It's great to know we can celebrate and praise GOD before something greater happens. Let us leap for joy!

WHAT DO YOU DO WHEN YOU'RE PREGNANT BUT CAN'T DELIVER?

Union Spring Church was originally located in Catuna, Louisiana. But this place was too small for the vision GOD gave. So, on September 8, 2008, the Union Spring Church congregation broke ground for a new place of worship downtown in the city of Mansfield. It was an old Ford Motors dealership property on about two acres. We were so excited to be in the city. As we broke ground that day, our hopes were up. We knew we were well on our way. We were pregnant with GOD's promise. It had been prophesied many times about our move to the city.

We began to tear down the old building and build our new edifice. Just as we got started, things happened that caused delays. People started to speak against our ministry. We still believed that we were pregnant with destiny, but we couldn't deliver. We needed help! We spent $250,000 just to start the process, we were threatening a miscarriage. We needed help! We begin to P.U.S.H. This is the acronym for *Pray Until Something Happens.* We cried, we prayed. Then we cried and prayed some more. Lord, what do we do now? We were at a standstill. No one would finance this project for us to continue to build. The next year in September, the church body went on a consecration fast for seven days still believing that GOD would deliver our overdue baby. After fasting and praying for those seven days, our faith was renewed. We knew it would happen but didn't know when.

It was the year 2015. GOD opened a door for an even greater place in the city for our church family to worship! This property came with seven acres. We moved in on the first Sunday in December of that year. The plan was to lease the property until we could formally close on it. Just as we thought we were about to close on it, we found a lien on the property for one million dollars. All I could say was "Lord, what do we do now"? We had already leased our property in Catuna to another ministry. We had nowhere to go. GOD told me not to share any of this information with the members, not even all the officers. We continued to lease this property not knowing the outcome. All we knew is that we were destined for this. Almost two years later, we own the property! Praise the Lord!

It took us from 2008 until November 8, 2017 to close on a new property in the city of Mansfield, Louisiana, that we could call our own. Pregnant with purpose, we had some trying times and so much pain. *Nine* years after the breaking of the ground, the water broke, and we delivered!

During these transitions we almost lost all our properties, but GOD made a way. This is a testament to what I know GOD can do.

So, for any pastor or business owner reading this please know that if you believe GOD and trust the process you will see victory. Allow GOD to lead you and when adversity comes, look out for the blessing in disguise. I am a witness you can't see the blessing in the eye of the storm, but you can trust in your heart that there is a bigger purpose taking place. When the dust settles, you can look back and see how the hand of GOD worked miracles on your behalf.

    I encourage you to keep going, keep believing, keep trusting, and keep the faith! Your latter shall be greater. You will succeed and conquer your fears with the help of GOD. Your vision will manifest, and help lives. The resources you need will show up! The Holy Spirit of GOD will accompany you to the delivery room so when it's time to push the vision, all the help you need will be in place. Begin to thank GOD now that you are on schedule and in route to birth GREATNESS into the earth! Your Help is here!

www.ingramcontent.com/pod-product-compliance
Lightning Source LLC
Chambersburg PA
CBHW070737020526
44118CB00035B/1430